PHILOSOPHICAL
ANALYSIS

PHILOSOPHICAL ANALYSIS

ITS DEVELOPMENT BETWEEN
THE TWO WORLD WARS

BY

J. O. URMSON

STUDENT OF CHRIST CHURCH AND
LECTURER IN PHILOSOPHY IN THE
UNIVERSITY OF OXFORD

OXFORD
AT THE CLARENDON PRESS
1956

Oxford University Press, Amen House, London E.C.4

GLASGOW NEW YORK TORONTO MELBOURNE WELLINGTON
BOMBAY CALCUTTA MADRAS KARACHI CAPE TOWN IBADAN

Geoffrey Cumberlege, Publisher to the University

———

PRINTED IN GREAT BRITAIN

CONTENTS

PART III

THE BEGINNINGS OF CONTEMPORARY PHILOSOPHY

INTRODUCTION

AMONG the philosophers who were most influential in England in the period between the two world wars were the analysts. Their analytic theories were sometimes associated with the metaphysical view which Russell called logical atomism, sometimes with the supposedly anti-metaphysical doctrines of logical positivism, and sometimes, as in the case of G. E. Moore, the analytic practice had no clearly defined dogmatic background at all. But they were united at least in the view that analysis was at least one of the most important tasks of the philosopher; and by analysis they meant something which, whatever precise description of it they chose, at least involved the attempt to rewrite in different and in some way more appropriate terms those statements which they found philosophically puzzling. In the later thirties some analysts had become dissatisfied with this conception of their task and a new view of philosophical method, together with a new philosophical practice, was being evolved; but they were few in number and their ideas had not had time to become widely disseminated or understood when the war broke out.

During the years of the war public philosophizing was practically at a standstill in England, though a few important articles in the new style were published. Yet during these years many analytic philosophers quietly assimilated and developed these new ideas and discarded the old; and when they returned to philosophy after the war they returned to philosophize in the new style without any formal recantation or explanation. The result has been that many people with a good knowledge of the philosophical views and methods current between the wars have found themselves totally unable to understand post-war developments; on the other hand, many younger students of philosophy, brought up in the newer ways, have but the vaguest ideas about how their philosophical methods evolved from the older methods.

This book is therefore intended to serve two purposes. The first is to explain how the general attitude towards philosophy and the philosophical method typical of the post-war period in England were formed; the second is to give a picture of the historical background of this attitude and method. To put it another way, the aim is both to make later developments intelligible to those who are fairly well acquainted with the past but are puzzled by these developments, and also to give some account of the background of these later methods to those who are familiar with them but are unclear how they came to be adopted.

It is no part of the purpose of this book to give a full history of philosophy in the period between the wars; only the analytic movement which is particularly associated with the names of Russell, Moore, Wittgenstein, Ramsey, Wisdom, all Cambridge men, and with the Vienna Circle, represented in England most powerfully by Ayer, will be discussed in anything more than a casual way, for it is the influence of this group which was of paramount importance in stimulating that present-day approach which I shall try to make more intelligible. The work of even these philosophers will not be examined in detail; only their general method of work and attitude towards philosophy will be discussed, and then always from such a viewpoint and in such proportions as is likely to illuminate subsequent work. Any discussion of the views of these philosophers on more specialized topics will therefore be for illustrative purposes only and will be developed only so far as those purposes warrant.

Neither philosophy nor its history can be studied in paraphrase and précis. A satisfactory understanding of the methods of analysis used between the wars can be gained only from the original documents, and no attempt is made here to provide a second best to this but rather to give anyone who wishes to study these documents sufficient information to enable him to do so in a purposeful and methodical way. Without such guidance the large literature on the subject in books and journals cannot be profitably tackled. The danger of the generalized and composite outline given here is that the impression may be formed that there was a definite school, with an orthodoxy of its own, consciously moving from position to position as difficulties in the 'received' view were noticed and amendments sanctioned. Such an impression would, of course, be utterly mistaken; it should be easily discounted by any reader, who must know that in philosophy as the term is here understood there are no schools, creeds, and orthodoxies. But it would be hypersensitive to allow the fact of individual variety of view to obscure the fact that a general pattern of thought can be discerned, which it is helpful to examine both as a preliminary to the more detailed study of the views of individual philosophers and as a background against which the present can be better understood. That will be our object.

Apart, then, from the inevitable simplifications which my composite picture entails, I believe that a reliable account of the matter is given here. But one important qualification must be made to this claim. In the light of later study, aided by posthumous publication of Wittgenstein's writings, many philosophers have come to doubt the accuracy of the sort of interpretation of Wittgenstein's *Tractatus Logico-philosophicus* that is given here; in particular they would claim that the orientation of his thought was much more to logical and less to epistemological problems than is here suggested—for example, his *Sachverhalten* would be regarded as more akin to logical possibilities than to Russell's atomic facts. These doubts may well be justified. The excuse that must be offered for disregard of them here is that it was the sort of interpretation I have given, right or wrong, which was accepted in the period under examination, and which has therefore been of historical importance and influence. For our purposes it is what Wittgenstein was thought to mean that matters. It would have been an intolerable complication in a book which is not a specialist account of Wittgenstein's thought to have given in detail both the received and influential version of his views and in addition a new interpretation which philosophers have only begun to work out in the past few years.

The general plan is as follows: after a sketch of a still earlier background, a picture of the analytic movement in its hey-day will be given, together with its complementary metaphysics of logical atomism; this is the period, roughly, from 1919 to 1934. An account then follows of the logical positivism, already developed in Vienna, which replaced logical atomism as a focus of interest, though few embraced it whole-heartedly; together with this the revised view of the nature of analysis which went with logical positivism is examined. Next, some account is given of those few articles which appeared shortly before war began in 1939 which serve as a foretaste of what was to follow. In a final retrospect a short analysis of the fundamental causes of the changes of view which were gradually accomplished during the whole period under review will be offered.

A list of principal works to which reference is made is appended; it may be of aid as an indication of the scope of this book.

world. The swing of the pendulum from this monism, with its doctrine of internal relations, largely accounts, so far as historical causation goes (we must not think that we are dealing with a simple emotional reaction), for the radical pluralism of the atomists, signalized by Russell calling himself a logical atomist, and by the sustained attacks on the doctrine of internal relations.

Secondly, logical atomism was a reaction against an extreme realism which had replaced the philosophy of Bradley for both Moore and Russell. In his article 'The Nature of Judgement', published in *Mind* in 1899, Moore had argued that in judgement the mind was contemplating a wholly independent concept, which Bradley unduly psychologized (e.g. the judgement that lions exist involves the simultaneous contemplation of the non-mental concepts of lionhood and existence), and in the famous 'Refutation of Idealism' he claimed that the idealists had by a verbal play confused the wholly independent object of sense (which can be called a sensation) with the sensation which is part of our mental history. Russell, who accepted these arguments of Moore and was also influenced by what he then considered to be the metaphysical and epistemological requirements for the explanation of the nature and validity of mathematics, went more or less the whole way with Meinong in the acceptance of a shadow-world of being, including essentially numbers, classes, and propositions, but containing, as an inevitable corollary, much more besides. Lest readers better acquainted with the later Russell should suspect exaggeration, here is a quotation from Russell[1] at this period:

Being is that which belongs to every conceivable term, to every possible object of thought—in short to everything that can possibly occur in any proposition, true or false, and to all such propositions themselves. Being belongs to whatever can be counted. If *A* be any term that can be counted as one, it is plain that *A* is

[1] *Principles of Mathematics*, para. 427.

PART I

PHILOSOPHICAL ANALYSIS AND LOGICAL ATOMISM

1

THE HISTORICAL BACKGROUND OF LOGICAL ATOMISM

BEFORE we start on our more detailed investigations of the beginnings of logical atomism, which might be arbitrarily dated at the publication of Russell's *Our Knowledge of the External World* in 1914, some consideration must be given to the philosophical developments which led up to it. But there is no one correct point at which to start; one cannot understand Russell properly without some knowledge of Bradley, who again can only be fully understood in the light of his reaction to Mill and his followers, and so on through a regress to the beginnings of philosophical speculation. We must break in arbitrarily somewhere.

Russell and Moore, the co-founders of the analytic movement, were at first in reaction against Bradley and the Neo-Hegelian philosophers, a reaction only the stronger because both Moore and Russell had been admirers and, more or less, followers of Bradley in their philosophical youth. In Bradley they found the idea of the world as a single, indivisible whole, the attempted isolation of any element in which involves distortion and partial falsehood; there are no self-contained facts short of Reality as a whole—the Absolute. This position was reached by a process of *a priori* reasoning, which professed to find contradictions in any other view of the something, and therefore that A is. 'A is not' must always be either false or meaningless. For if A were nothing, it could not be said not to be; 'A is not' implies that there is a term A whose being is denied, and hence that A is. Thus unless 'A is not' be an empty sound, it must be false—whatever A may be, it certainly is. Numbers, the Homeric gods, relations, chimeras and four-dimensional spaces all have being, for if they were not entities of a kind, we could make no propositions about them. Thus being is a general attribute of everything, and to mention anything is to show that it is.

The most obvious existing alternative to atomism was the form of empiricism which had been revived by John Stuart Mill. But Bradley, who was castigated by Moore for being too psychological, had himself made the subjective psychologism of Mill and his followers the main point of his attack on them; in any case Mill's empiricist theory of mathematics repelled Russell. Since Moore and Russell were moving towards a highly realistic pluralism it was clearly impossible for them to go back to Mill. They were in fact reacting against both the monism of the idealists and the subjectivism of contemporary empiricism.

As the quotation from Russell amply shows, the reaction against monism had occurred in a way which had led to what the robust common sense of Moore and Russell was soon to stigmatize as a far too indiscriminate pluralism. Apart, therefore, from the reaction against monism, it was mainly as a means for dealing with classes, numbers, propositions, chimeras, and so on, intended to avoid both the confusion and obscurity of conceptualism, and also the nightmare underworld of a more than Platonic realism, that the analytic method which is the object of our investigation was evolved. It is important to remember that Russell, so important in the history of analytical philosophy, had been successively under the influence of Bradley and the extreme realism of Meinong, and in turn rejected them; for it was the errors of these views, naturally enough, that he and his followers were afterwards most concerned to avoid. He was on guard against the errors of Bradley and Meinong as we are against his. It is the errors that we have once embraced that we see most clearly and most carefully seek to avoid.

As a matter of history, the weapons which Russell used to demolish the superfluous parts of his swollen world of being were created by him before he developed the general theory of logical atomism. But as they were at first developed with an eye to and used in solving the problems of mathematical logic, we shall consider them in the later context of logical atomism where they received a more general employment. These weapons were the theory of descriptions and the method of logical constructions. It would be wrong, of course, to suggest that Russell started on his mathematical researches as an extreme realist and on his first return to general philosophical problems was already a fully-fledged logical atomist. But Russell has left so easily readable and well-known an account of an intermediate position in his *Problems of Philosophy* of 1912 that it would be superfluous to recapitulate here the gradual development of his views.

It would be a mistake to think that, because in his logical atomism Russell and those he influenced were reacting against Bradley's monism and the realism which he had accepted from Moore, Meinong, and Frege, the analytic movement which we are now to study was in its earlier form predominantly anti-metaphysical. Logical atomism was presented as a superior metaphysics which was to replace inferior ones, not as an attack on metaphysics as such. Indeed, as presented in the documents of its hey-day, logical atomism is one of the most thorough-going metaphysical systems yet elaborated. This is true in spite of the anti-metaphysical strain which is to be found in Wittgenstein's *Tractatus Logico-philosophicus*, alongside of the metaphysics. For breadth of sweep, clarity, detailed working-out, and consistency it can have few rivals.

Most similar to it of all the great metaphysical systems of the past is that of Leibniz, for whom Russell had a significant admiration.

Earlier views about the nature and purpose of philosophical analysis were so tied up with the metaphysics of logical atomism that it will be well to turn our attention first to the metaphysics before examining the analytic method with which it went in harness.

2

A PRELIMINARY SKETCH OF LOGICAL ATOMISM

A. METAPHYSICS AND LOGIC

MANY metaphysical systems which endeavour to give a general account of the world are clearly modelled on some less high-flying discipline. Thus it is in general clear, however obscure the details, that the Pythagoreans tried to give an account of the world in terms of their geometry; it is tempting to see Locke's metaphysics as a general application of atomistic mechanics; some modern metaphysicians have avowedly borrowed the conceptions of evolutionary biology; and so on. The shortest account of logical atomism that can be given is that the world has the structure of Russell's mathematical logic.

In the first of his articles in the *Monist* on logical atomism Russell said: 'The kind of philosophy that I wish to advocate, which I call logical atomism, is one which has forced itself upon me in the course of thinking about the philosophy of mathematics . . . I shall try to set forth . . . a certain kind of logical doctrine and on the basis of this a certain kind of metaphysics.'

This quotation well illustrates the fact that both Russell and Wittgenstein, who was originally his pupil, came to the problems of general philosophy from the study of mathematical logic and the philosophy of mathematics. Russell's great problem had been to construct a logic by means of which he could derive from the smallest possible number of purely logical notions and axioms, and no others, the whole of mathematics, thereby exhibiting the continuity of mathematics and logic. To carry out this task he had, with his collaborator Whitehead, constructed a logic very much richer, and with incomparably more powerful techniques, than any before known.

Let us first state in two or three sentences how this new, rich logic suggested a whole philosophical position to Russell, as he said it did in the passage quoted above. This summary statement must inevitably be cryptic and inadequate, but may none the less be a useful signpost to what is to follow. Russell, it appears, considered that a logic from which the whole of mathematics with all its complexities can be derived must be an adequate skeleton (minus the extra-logical vocabulary which the variables replace) of a language capable of expressing all that can be accurately said at all. Holding, too, that 'the study of grammar is capable of throwing far more light on philosophical questions than is commonly supposed by philosophers',[1] he came to think that the world would have the structure of this logic, whose grammar was so perfect, unlike that of the misleading natural languages. As the logic had individual variables in its vocabulary, so the world would contain a variety of particulars, the names of which would be constants to replace, as extra-logical vocabulary, these variables; as the logic required only extensional, truth-functional, connectives between its elementary propositions, so the world would consist of independent, extensionally connected facts; as the techniques of logic could define and thus make theoretically superfluous the more complex and abstruse concepts of mathematics, so, by the application of the same techniques the less concrete items of the furniture of heaven and earth, the Meinongian underworld, could be defined and theoretically eliminated. The structure of the world would thus resemble the structure of *Principia Mathematica*. That is the simple argument of the plot.

Since the metaphysics is thus dependent on the logic, it is clearly indispensable to have some sort of understanding of

[1] *Principles of Mathematics*, para. 46.

what sort of logic it is and of the concepts it employs if we are to understand the metaphysics. For our purposes the more advanced and difficult parts of the logic are luckily less important than the most simple and no reference need be made to them. Since a knowledge of logic cannot be assumed, a highly informal account of the concept of a truth-function and allied concepts of the sentential calculus follows; being an informal (and short) account of a formal matter it will of necessity be imprecise. Any reader who needs and wishes to do so can supplement it from any modern introduction to logic.

B. THE GENERAL NATURE OF THE LOGIC OF TRUTH-FUNCTIONS

Any statement (proposition) may be true or false; formal logic presupposes this and the existence of extra-logical ways of finding out whether they are true or false (e.g. by observation). Since the logician wishes to talk indifferently about all statements whatever their content or structure, he does not mention any specific statements, but uses instead variables, as they are called, p, q, r, &c., which stand in the place of any possible statement, it does not matter which. Thus if the logician asks us to consider the conjunction 'p and q' he is in effect asking us to consider the conjunction of any two statements, no matter what they say. If he were to say, for example, that 'p and q' is true if and only if p and q are separately true, he would be in effect saying that if you conjoin any two statements whatsoever, this conjunction will be true if and only if the conjoined statements are severally true.

Let us first consider any two statements p and q, taken for the purpose of logic as ones whose truth or falsehood can be determined extra-logically; we might, for example, take 'he is old' and 'he is tired'. By means of logical connectives we can form a single complex statement out of these two. By the use of the logical connective 'and' we may get the conjunction 'p and q' ('he is old and he is tired'); by the use of the logical

connective 'or' we may get 'p or q' ('he is old or he is tired').
By the introduction of negation we can also produce many
more complex statements containing p and q, thus: 'not-p
and not-q' ('he is not old and he is not tired'), 'p or not-q' ('he
is old or he is not tired'), and so on. Still more simply we can
regard the negation 'not-p' as a complex statement containing
p. If we wish to know whether any of these statements which
we have formed by means of negation and logical connectives
is true or false, it seems evident that all we need to know is
whether p and q taken separately are true or false. If we know
that p is true, we know that not-p is false; if we know that p
is false and that q is true, we can easily see that 'p and q' is
false, 'not-p and q' is true and 'p or q' is true. As the content of
p and of q is irrelevant we are clearly justified in treating them
as variables, which may be replaced by any statements, and
not merely as abbreviations for 'he is old' and 'he is tired'.

It is clear that the addition of a third variable r, or of a
fourth, or fifth, or any number of variables, makes no theoretical difference. Thus 'p and q and r' is true if and only if all
three are true, and 'p or q or r' is true if and only if at least one
of the three is true.

We can now define the very important expression 'truth-
function'. When the truth or falsity of a complex statement
can be determined solely from the truth and falsity of its
constituent statements it is called a truth-function of its constituent statements. Thus 'he is old and he is tired' is a truth-
function of 'he is old' and 'he is tired'; 'p or q' is a truth-function
of p and q; 'not-p' is a truth function of p; and so on.

In formal logic the connectives 'and' and 'or' are always
given a minimum meaning, as we have done above, such that
any complex formed by the use of them alone is a truth-
function of its constituents. In ordinary discourse the connectives often have a richer meaning; thus 'he took off his
clothes and went to bed' implies temporal succession and has
a different meaning from 'he went to bed and took off his

clothes'. Logicians would justify their use of the minimum meaning by pointing out that it is the common element in all our uses of 'and'.

It should be noted that the connectives 'and' and 'or' are, with the aid of negation, interdefinable, so that one could be theoretically eliminated. Thus 'he is old and he is tired' is clearly different from 'he is old or he is tired'; but 'he is old and he is tired' can be replaced by 'It is not the case that either he is not old or he is not tired' without change of meaning; in symbols $(p$ and $q) = $ not-(not-p or not-q).

Most truth-functions which we can construct will be in some circumstances true and in others false, depending on which of the constituents we regard as true and which as false. This holds of all the examples we have so far considered. Thus 'he is old or he is tired' will be false if he is young and brimming with energy, otherwise it will be true. Since logicians have no means within their discipline of determining the truth or falsity of the constituents of their truth functions, they have no means of determining the truth or falsity of these truth-functions which may be true or may be false; therefore as logicians they have little interest in them. But there are two other sorts of truth-function which are of special interest to the logician which must be noticed.

(i) The truth-function 'p or not-p' is a function of the single constituent p. It is a truth-function of p since its truth can be determined by a knowledge of the truth or falsity of this constituent. But in this case we can see that it is true whether the constituent be true or false—its truth can be logically determined. Similarly it is easy to see that the truth-function '(p and q) or (not-p or not-q)' is a logical truth, since it will be true in all the four conceivable circumstances of (a) p and q both true, (b) p true, q false, (c) p false, q true, (d) p and q both false. Truth-functions which are true for all possibilities of truth and falsehood of their constituents are called tautologies.

(ii) Similarly it is possible to construct truth-functions

which are false, irrespective of the truth or falsehood of their constituents, such as 'p and not-p'. Such truth-functions are called contradictions.

The main interest of truth-functions for the formal logician is to spot which of them are tautologies and to devise ways of proving whether any given function, however complicated, is a tautology; Russell's method was to start with some tautologies as axioms and prove as theorems that other functions were also tautologies. Since then other much neater techniques have been invented, but as we shall be little concerned with the tautologies that interest formal logicians we need not go into this matter.

We may sum up the matter thus: the formal logician regards himself as supplied with an indefinite number of propositional variables, p, q, r, &c.; since he does not inquire into their structure we may say that they are simple relative to his system. By the use of negation and such logical connectives as 'and' and 'or' he then constructs truth-functions of these variables. Since he has no logical means of determining the truth or falsehood of the constituents he limits his interest to those of the functions which can be recognized to be true or false by logical methods—the tautologies and contradictions. Since it is the tautologies which are of importance for research into the foundations of mathematics, this suits him perfectly.

A calculus in which all complex propositions, i.e. propositions which are not simple relative to the system, are truth-functions is said to be truth-functional or extensional.

So much must suffice as an explanation of the ideas of elementary logic which were adapted for use in the metaphysics of logical atomism.

C. LANGUAGE AS TRUTH-FUNCTIONAL

Russell, it will be remembered, claimed that, used with caution, grammar can be a guide to the structure of reality.

On the basis of our short account of the apparatus of the logic of truth-functions we can now sketch more intelligibly the atomists' view of the structure of language. We shall give it first in the more extreme form in which it was held by Wittgenstein; we shall have occasion later to indicate some of the ways in which Russell differed from it.

As there are in the logic a host of variables p, q, r, &c., which are simple relative to the logic, Wittgenstein held that there must be a host of absolutely simple propositions in ordinary language, having no logical complexity. Any proposition containing 'ands' and 'ors' must ultimately consist of propositions which do not contain them. All other propositions of any language, he held, can be regarded as being truth-functions of these elementary propositions. Necessary truths will have the character of the tautologies of the logic, impossible propositions (such as 'it is raining and it is not raining') will have the character of the contradictions of the logic; and the remainder, including all the elementary propositions, will be empirical propositions corresponding to the truth-functions of logic which will be true in some conditions, false in others, and whose truth cannot be ascertained by logical means.

To put the matter shortly, Wittgenstein held that the artificial language of truth-functions was the skeleton of the language of ordinary discourse, though the true logical structure of language was often concealed by the *ad hoc* grammatical conventions we employ. This thesis that language is throughout truth-functional was often called the thesis of extensionality. Every statement anyone ever makes must, according to this thesis of extensionality, be either a logically simple statement or else a truth-function of such statements, even if some of the statements which are really truth-functions of a quite complicated kind are often given a conventional abbreviation.

Tautologies (necessary truths) and contradictions, it was held, tell us nothing about the world since they are compatible respectively with any or no possible state of affairs. To know whether other complex propositions are true it is indispensable to ascertain the truth or falsity of the elementary propositions of which they are truth-functions by observation or other empirical means. This is not the case with tautologies; but we know their truth not by any non-empirical insight into the facts but by seeing that they are compatible with all states of affairs, all combinations of the truth and falsehood of their elementary propositions, and hence cannot tell us anything false. They are offshoots of our symbolism which really tell us nothing and may be regarded as, in the mathematical sense, degenerate cases. Thus the mystery was taken out of our knowledge of necessary truth. Wittgenstein himself put the case succinctly as follows in the *Tractatus* (4.46, 4.461, 4.4611, 4.462):

4.46 Among the possible groups of truth-conditions there are two extreme cases.

In the one case a proposition is true for all the truth-possibilities of its elementary propositions. We say that the truth-conditions are *tautological*.

In the second case the proposition is false for all the truth-possibilities. The truth-conditions are *self-contradictory*.

In the first case we call the proposition a tautology, in the second a contradiction.

4.461 Propositions show what they say, tautologies and contradictions that they say nothing.

Tautologies have no truth-conditions, for they are unconditionally true; and contradictions are on no condition true.

Tautology and contradiction are without sense.

(Like the point from which two arrows go out in opposite directions.)

(I know nothing, e.g., about the weather, when I know that it is raining or not raining.)

4.4611 Tautology and contradiction are, however, not nonsensical; they belong to the symbolism in the same way that 'o' belongs to the symbolism of arithmetic.

4.462   Tautology and contradiction are not pictures of reality. They exhibit no possible state of affairs. For the one allows *every* possible state of affairs, the other *none*.

Clearly this view leads us to the problem of how there can be any point in pursuing mathematical and other deductive enterprises, if they are tautological in this way. The atomists were not unaware of this problem, but we cannot now examine their treatment of it. It is the non-tautological, non-contradictory truth-functions with which we shall be chiefly concerned.

This is, of course, but the baldest summary of an extreme form of the atomists' view of language as truth-functional or extensional, but before we begin to fill in the gaps it will perhaps be helpful to indicate in summary form how they made use of the thesis of extensionality as a clue to their metaphysical account of the nature of the world.

D. THE METAPHYSICAL APPLICATION OF THIS VIEW OF LANGUAGE

A language, we have seen, was conceived by the atomists as being basically an indefinitely large collection of simple, elementary, or, as it was often put, atomic propositions, the truth of which had to be settled by extra-logical, empirical methods; any statement which does not consist of a single atomic proposition is merely a truth-function of such atomic propositions, and its truth or falsity can be determined simply by determining the truth or falsity of the atomic propositions it contains. Therefore, in a sense, there is nothing to be said beyond what can be said in atomic propositions. But a proposition is made true by what we may at present vaguely call its correspondence with fact. Therefore the world must consist of an indefinitely large number of atomic facts to which the true atomic propositions will correspond; and as the atomic propositions are conceived as being logically independent, so these facts must be conceived as being metaphysically independent. Without such correspondence between language and fact it seemed to the logical atomists that it would be impossible to talk about the world at all. Just as any non-atomic proposition, a molecular proposition, can be regarded as an extensional or truth-functional combination of atomic propositions, so any non-atomic or molecular fact is nothing in itself beyond a group of atomic facts wholly independent of each other. To put the matter in a nutshell, if language consists essentially of nothing but atomic propositions there can be nothing to say about the world except to report in atomic propositions those atomic facts to which the atomic propositions correspond. As Wittgenstein put it in the first two main propositions of his *Tractatus Logico-philosophicus*, 'The world is everything that is the case. . . . What is the case, the fact, is the existence of atomic facts.'

Let us illustrate this view with a rather crude model. If we suppose that there are n significant atomic propositions, each of which states or fails to state an atomic fact, then a complete account of the world, all being said that there is to say, would be given by an enumeration of all the atomic propositions which do state an atomic fact, and the negation of all the rest of our n propositions. If, to take a particularly unreal example to illustrate the principle, there were only three possible atomic propositions, then we could give a complete account of the world by selecting one of the 2^3 possible states of affairs $p \& q \&\text{-}r$ or $p \& q \& r$, or $p \&\text{-}q \& r$, &c. Generally, if there are n atomic propositions, they yield 2^n possible worlds, of which a true and complete account of the world as it is would select one. There would be nothing further to say beyond this. Short of this ideal encyclopaedic knowledge, we can give a partial account of the world or else merely exclude some possibilities from the world—'p or q' will, for example, exclude the world which lacks both the atomic facts pictured by p and q, but does not select the world containing p or the world containing q. Any significant statement is therefore either the affirmation or the rejection of some atomic fact, or it affirms or rejects a conjunction or disjunction of such atomic facts; logic further shows that we have not two different possibilities in conjunction and disjunction, but only two alternative symbolisms. The world is thus taken to be of identical structure with, and to be perfectly representable by, a language with the structure of the logical language of *Principia Mathematica*, and even so, on this more extreme thesis of Wittgenstein, some of the symbolism of *Principia Mathematica*, such as the quantifiers, is theoretically superfluous.

That is the view of logic, and the metaphysical view which was derived from it, in the barest outline. The daring simplicity and the metaphysical boldness of it are surely immediately apparent. It does not seem to be entirely fanciful to see a similarity here to the views of Leibniz. To the monads correspond the basic facts; as the monads are windowless so the facts live in the splendid isolation of an extensional logic. There is, too, the intimate combination of logical with metaphysical theses, but we must not digress too far back in time.

Since one of our main interests is the development of methods of analysis it would not be appropriate to continue immediately with a detailed explanation and examination of all the details of the metaphysics of logical atomism for their own sake. But before we turn to the theory of analysis which went with this metaphysics our rough sketch must be amplified by some further discussion of two key conceptions; we must first give a more detailed account of what the atomists' view of atomic facts was; then we must explain what the relation between an atomic proposition and an atomic fact was conceived to be, that relation which we have so far vaguely indicated as correspondence, but which the atomists called picturing. Even on these points some details will be omitted for further discussion in Chapter 5.

(i) *Atomic facts*

The most general account given by the atomists of an atomic fact was that it was a fact consisting either in the possession by a particular of a characteristic or in a relation holding between two or more particulars. A fact in which a particular has some absolutely simple and determinate characteristic was known as a monadic fact. A fact in which two particulars are related by some absolutely simple and determinate relation was called a dyadic fact. When three particulars are so related we have a triadic fact. No upper limit can be set *a priori*. Generally, if *n* particulars are so related we have an *n*-adic fact. What then are these particulars? On that point let us first consider the statements of Russell in his articles in the *Monist* on logical atomism:

Particulars= terms of relations in atomic facts. Def.
Proper names = words for particulars. Def.
Particulars have this peculiarity, among the sorts of object that you have to take account of in an inventory of the world, that each of them stands alone and is completely self-subsistent.
Each particular that there is in the world does not in any way logically depend on any particular.

Taking a simple coloured patch (in the sense in which sense-datum theorists understand coloured patches) as the most likely candidate for the status of particular that he can think of, Russell also says: 'A particular as a rule is apt to last for a very short time indeed. . . . In that respect particulars differ from the old substances but in their logical position they do not.' It is important to see that in accordance with the derivation of the metaphysics from logic the atomists did not say that some particular things appeared to be the basic ingredients of the world from which they would try to build it, but decided *a priori* what the basic ingredients would be like, and then looked round for things to fill the bill; they never claimed with any dogmatism that any particular sort of thing did fill the bill. We cannot therefore give certain examples of atomic facts, but favourite illustrative examples were such as a particular sense-datum being of a certain shade (monadic fact) or adjoining another (dyadic fact) and so on. It would in fact be hard to deny that the ease with which logical atomism seemed to fit in with the sense-datum theory helped to secure it wider acceptance.

(ii) *Pictures of atomic facts*

We cannot at this stage discuss the problems raised by the vagaries of natural languages, but will confine ourselves to the question how an atomic proposition in a perfect language was envisaged as being related to the fact which it stated and to which it corresponded. Russell gave in his *Monist* articles the following first approximation to an answer: 'In a logically perfect language the words in a proposition would correspond one by one with the components of the corresponding fact.'

Russell also held that in a perfect language there would be a single word to denote each simple object or particular and many to denote each complex: 'A language of that sort', he claimed, 'will show at a glance the logical structure of the fact asserted or denied.'

In thus speaking of a perfect language Russell did not consider himself as being utopian; as we have already seen, he claimed that *Principia Mathematica* contained the skeleton of just such a language, though it lacked the flesh of a vocabulary. To give it flesh the Greek letters ϕ and ψ would have to be replaced by the names of such characteristics as the context required; similarly the Rs would have to be replaced by names of relations and the as and bs by names of particulars. Thus, for example, all such propositions as 'This white' which state monadic facts would be of the skeletal type ϕa; of the form aRb we should have such propositions as 'This next that', stating dyadic facts. All authorities agreed that such forms of words as 'This is white' and 'This is next to that' would not do because the word 'is' was superfluous. The other words in the sentences named some element in the fact, but there was no extra element for the word 'is' to name; its introduction was an imperfection of the English language, which it shared not even with all natural languages.

But the most strenuous and subtle seekers after perfection doubted seriously whether ordinary language could be made as perfect as *Principia Mathematica* by such simple devices as omission of the verb 'to be'. For if we consider such a sentence as 'This red', even in the favourable circumstances when there is some genuine particular which is red to be talked of, the following difficulties arise: (1) it is not certain that in ordinary language 'this' is a genuine logically proper name; it may be the abbreviation of a description meaning something like 'the thing I am pointing at'. Then we shall be doubly at fault, for we shall be passing off a complex description as a name and also representing a complex description by a single word. (2) It is not certain that 'red' names, as is required in a perfect language, a completely determinate shade or only a shade within certain vague boundaries. In the latter case 'red' will not name an element in the fact, and similar difficulties to those set out in (1) above will arise.

But (3) another difficulty of a more interesting kind also arose which will only be indicated now and more fully discussed in Chapter 5. Russell, in the symbolism of his formal logic, uses, in addition to many other devices, two different types of letters; on the one hand, ordinary lower-case letters, on the other, Greek letters such as ϕ and ψ and the capital R. The function of these two types of symbol can be indicated by saying that if we were to replace these variables by a non-logical vocabulary the lower-case letters would give place to names of particulars, the Greek letters to names of characteristics, and the capital R to names of relations. Thus in the symbolic expression ϕa we could replace the ϕ by 'red' and the a by 'this', to get the statement

'This (is) red'. In accordance with the view that the world contains two irreducibly different kinds of things, usually called universals and particulars, Russell called the universal elements in facts components of those facts and the particular elements he called constituents of the facts. So we see that the difference in type of symbol was intended to indicate whether the symbol named a component or constituent, ordinary lower-case letters standing for constituents and the capital R and the Greek letters for components. In Russell's view every proposition must contain one symbol at least of each type and every fact must contain at least one component and one constituent. The objection raised was that at least in the case of ordinary language we use words of the same type to represent both the constituent and the component; thus a relation between two particulars will be very inadequately represented by three similar-looking words side by side, as in the case of the sentence 'this next that'. It was considered that even Russell's symbolism was inadequate to the facts, the mere use of a different kind of type not showing adequately the immense gulf between the logical characteristics of components and constituents. A very special doctrine of the nature of the perfect language was hinted at by Wittgenstein in the *Tractatus* and later developed by Wisdom to enable both the difference between constituents and components and also their intimate connexion to be adequately exhibited.

We cannot now pursue these questions of comparative detail farther. It is to be hoped that enough has been said to show that ideally the relation between statement and fact stated was one of formal or structural identity; it was this relation which made it seem appropriate to some of the analysts to speak of statements as pictures of facts. The form of a well-constructed symbolism could be thought by Russell to be a clue to the structure of the world precisely because what made it a well-constructed symbolism was its similarity of structure to the reality that it portrayed. The aim of analysis thus was to make every statement an adequate picture of the reality it referred to, and the perfect language was the tool which could make the undertaking capable of complete realization.

3

ATOMISTIC METAPHYSICS AND ANALYSIS

WE have still a great deal more to say by way of amplification before we can claim to have provided an adequate picture of logical atomism. But we have so far presented the metaphysics as a set of bare assertions without any ground for acceptance; and we have not indicated at all the connexion of the metaphysics with the analytic method the development of which we are mainly concerned to trace. It will therefore be advisable to interrupt our metaphysical exegesis at this point in order to try to show how the metaphysics was connected with analytic practice and why the metaphysics was accepted, in particular why the identity of structure of at least an ideal language and reality was so strongly insisted upon.

It will be possible to carry out these two investigations simultaneously because, as we shall find, the metaphysics commended itself largely as the rationale of the view of language and analysis with which it was conjoined. The method of analysis we shall find to be derived largely from the application to general epistemological problems of the theory of descriptions and the doctrine of logical constructions which Russell had developed in his investigation of the foundations of mathematics in the period immediately preceding the formulation of the metaphysics of atomism.

Let us start again from the views of Meinong and the Russell of the *Principles of Mathematics* and consider the statement that the round square is impossible. What is impossible?—the round square, apparently. What then is this round square? Nothing existent, clearly, since it is impossible. But it is not just *nothing*; we are certainly saying that something is impossible; we cannot leave a blank in place of the words 'round square'. Is it then an idea in our heads, the idea of a round square, that we are declaring to be impossible? Surely not; we are not saying that any idea is impossible. Again, suppose someone says 'This is yellow'; then if we cannot locate the *this*, if there is no *this*, the statement will be unintelligible. By parity of reasoning, it would appear, there must in some sense be a round square, since we can understand 'The round square is impossible'. It does not, it was agreed, exist, nor does it subsist in the manner of abstract entities, but it must have some sort of being, some ontological status. In some such way as this both Russell and Meinong had argued. Maybe the conclusion will be unacceptable to a robust common sense; but the problem, age-old in its essentials, is one which required a solution, and which could not be simply thrust aside.

Russell, in the course of his mathematical inquiries, had already produced an alternative solution to this problem, and a host of similar ones, which, though it has recently come under attack, was for long regarded as a paradigm of philosophy, and which may well be such even if not finally accurate. This solution was first given by Russell in his article 'On Denoting' which was published in *Mind* in 1905 and was developed in the various statements of his theory of descriptions. We cannot here recapitulate the whole of this theory in an accurate form, but some essential points may be noted. Traditional logic had been wrong, Russell claimed, in assimilating propositions of the form 'The so and so is B' (such as 'The carpet in the hall is red') to propositions of the form 'This is B' (such as 'This is red'), symbolizing them both by 'This A is B'. 'This is B', where 'this' is a logically proper name, is a genuine singular proposition which will indeed be unintelligible if there is nothing that 'this' can refer to. But 'The so and so is B', however similar in grammatical appearance, is logically quite different; it is in fact a general proposition, not a singular one. Thus 'The King of France is bald', prima facie puzzling in the absence of a King of France, should be read in some such way as 'There is something which is both King of France and bald, and only one such thing'. The final clause is necessary because the definite article implies that there is only one; if the indefinite article be substituted in the original the clause can be omitted. Thus translated the proposition is simply the (false) claim that a definite description has an application when it has not, and the apparent need for a queer entity which shall be a non-existent King of France has gone. In this way then we can eliminate the puzzling uses of such phrases as 'the so and so' or 'a so and so', and at the same time show that what was in appearance a singular proposition is in fact general. There are stricter formulations of the theory than this from the point of view of logic. In 'On Denoting' Russell also gave reasons for preferring this account to another which Frege had given in his article 'On Sense and Reference'.[1]

Russell, then, had discovered a type of analysis which immediately recommended itself as abolishing some of the less desirable entities which it had previously been necessary to admit. But it is not the intrinsic interest of the theory which now particularly concerns us. We must note that Russell claimed, and the claim was very plausible, that it was more appropriate to write sentences beginning 'There is one and only one thing which . . .' than with definite descriptions 'The so and so . . .'. But why is this more appropriate? Perhaps we shall be told that it is less misleading? But how is it less misleading? What is right about it that is unsatisfactory in the usual formulation? It is an answer to this question to say that it is less misleading because it shows, pictures, reveals the form of the fact which the other formulation obscures; it has a structure more appropriate to the fact because it is at least more nearly similar to the structure of the fact. Philosophers nowadays, it is true, do not like this

[1] Reprinted in *Frege Translations*, edited by Black and Geach.

answer; but if they do not they must either give up preferring some formulations to others or else produce an alternative explanation of and ground for their preference. Philosophers of all persuasions are continually recasting sentences in what they regard as a better form, and if as philosophers we are going to do this we must have a reason for doing so. One of the reasons given by the atomists was that they were trying to picture better the form of the fact. Again, if we are to speak at all of logical form, we must say what we mean by this, as, for example, when we say that propositions containing definite descriptions are, in logical form, general. By postulating a world of facts having a structure similar to those of the expressions of logic and reformed language which did not mislead, and having the same purely extensional connexions as the propositions of their logic, the atomists provided themselves with an answer to this problem. Most philosophers who continue to make use of formal logic in the solution of philosophical problems, and continue to talk of the logical form of non-logical propositions, have no alternative statement of what they mean by this to offer, even when they reject the atomists' explanation. Thus we begin to see atomism as the rationale of the practice of analysis, which in part it was.

We may also note here that the theory of descriptions helps to explain the emphasis of the atomists on the need for single words which are logically proper names in the atomic propositions; for we can see that according to this theory a sentence containing a descriptive phrase is always general and thus could never picture uniquely one atomic fact.

Thus Russell's theory of descriptions, which commended itself on general epistemological and logical grounds, is a rule for analysis of a general kind for which logical atomism can be seen as a partial justification. But in a way, obviously circular but no less persuasive on that account, the metaphysical theory in its turn suggested a method and programme of analysis. If one reads, for example, Wittgenstein's account of a world consisting of atomic facts, each pictured by atomic sentences in a purely truth-functional language, one's first reaction is to say, with the statements of everyday language in mind, that it certainly does not sound as though this thesis is true. Wittgenstein, of course, knew this very well. He said in the *Tractatus* (4.002–4.0031):

> Everyday language is a part of the human organism and not less complicated than it. From it it is humanly impossible to gather immediately the logic of language. Language disguises the thought; so that from the external form of the clothes one cannot infer the form of the thought they clothe, because the external form of the clothes is constructed with quite another object than to let the form of the body be recognised. The tacit conventions for the understanding of everyday language are enormously complicated. . . . Most questions and propositions result from the fact that we do not understand the logic of our language. . . . It is a merit of Russell's to have shown that the apparent logical form of the proposition need not be its real form.

In other words, if logical atomism is right then logical analysis is a necessity. It is a necessity polemically in that unless the translation into something like the perfect language posited by the atomist is carried out in some crucial, illustrative cases, people will have very little reason to believe in the metaphysics of atomism; and it is a philosophical necessity since only by such a translation can the atomists find out for themselves the structure of the facts, and it is thus the only route to that clearer understanding of the world which is the object of metaphysics. Wisdom spoke the thought of them all when he said in one of his articles[1] that if a sentence F expresses the fact F' then the object of analysing the sentence F is to get 'clearer insight into the ultimate structure of F''. Wisdom added: 'Philosophic progress does not consist in acquiring knowledge of new facts but in acquiring new knowledge of facts —a passage *via* inspection from poor insight to good insight.'

[1] 'Logical Constructions', *Mind*, 1933, p. 195.

Thus logical atomism was regarded as acceptable because it gave an explanation of what was involved in the recasting of statements by philosophers, which is the form that analysis took at this period. The world has the form of its logically correct description discovered by the metaphysician by means of analysis. Further, by assigning the discovery of the forms of facts as the special problem of metaphysics, some solution was given to the ancient problem of what the metaphysician was doing better than spinning fairy-tales in an arm-chair while the scientist observed in his laboratory—he was gaining new knowledge of facts, not knowledge of new facts. Conversely, the atomist must engage in analysis if language is not to appear, on his own premiss of the identity of structure of language and fact, to give the lie to atomism.

However, analysis of the kind that is typified by the theory of descriptions may reasonably be said not to require a fully-fledged theory of logical atomism; equally, logical atomism seems to require other more profound types of analysis. For Russell had said of logical atomism in the *Monist* in 1919 that it was the view 'that you can get down in theory, if not in practice, to ultimate simples, out of which the world is built, and that these simples have a kind of reality not belonging to anything else'. But, it may be said, the kind of analysis exemplified by Russell's theory of descriptions requires at the most that we recognize that facts have a certain structure, which this analysis seeks to reveal, not that there are some more basic facts whose ingredients are simples having a different kind of reality from the common run. This is correct; our account of the theory of analysis which was held by the atomists is not yet complete even in outline. This lacuna must now be filled.

A. DIFFERENT TYPES OF ANALYSIS

It is clear that the kind of analysis exemplified by Russell's theory of descriptions has no close relation to the atomists' doctrine of basic facts. It can be applied in the same way to statements about 'the red sense-datum' and 'the average Englishman', and gives no support to the view that one refers to more basic facts than the other; in each case the descriptive phrase is to be eliminated by the same method. But analysis of a different type which does seem to give some justification for distinguishing different levels of fact was also recognized by the atomists. We must now try to show what these two types of analysis were and how they differed. The task is undeniably made more difficult by the confusion in Russell's use of terminology, particularly of the expression 'incomplete symbol', a confusion which seems to have concealed from Russell for a time the fact that more than one type of analysis was involved.

Russell introduced the expression 'incomplete symbol' in Chapter III of *Principia Mathematica*. He said: 'By an incomplete symbol we mean a symbol which is not supposed to have any meaning in isolation, but is only defined in certain contexts.' As examples he gave the mathematical symbols for differentiation and integration and definite descriptions (phrases like 'the so and so'). 'Such symbols', he said, 'have what may be called a "definition in use".' By this he means that rules can be given for the use of the expression in certain specified sorts of context, but that it is idle to ask what the expression in isolation stands for, and gives as an example of a definition in use the symbolic version of his analysis of definite descriptions in which he gives a meaning to 'the so and so is of such and such a kind' but gives no meaning to 'the so and so' in isolation. 'This', he said, 'distinguishes such symbols from what (in a generalized sense) we may call *proper names*; "Socrates", for example, stands for a certain man, and therefore has a meaning by itself, without the need of any context. If we supply a context, as in "Socrates is mortal", these words express a fact of which Socrates himself is a constituent.'

So far is relatively plain sailing; we have had the expression 'incomplete symbol' introduced in such a way that whenever by logical analysis we can eliminate an expression, as Russell eliminated descriptions by logical analysis, such an expression is to be called an incomplete symbol, and is regarded as having a meaning only in certain contexts. Since we can rephrase by analysis 'The master of Plato is mortal' in some such way as 'There is one and only one thing which is master of Plato and mortal', eliminating the apparent subject term 'the master of Plato', and merely leaving 'master of Plato' as a predicative expression, we can say that the definite description is an incomplete symbol: and since, as Russell here claims, the name 'Socrates' cannot be so eliminated, it is not an incomplete symbol.

But Russell puzzlingly adds:

The symbols for classes, like those for descriptions, are, in our system, incomplete symbols; their *uses* are defined, but they themselves are not assumed to mean anything at all. That is to say, the uses of such symbols are so defined that, when the *definiens* is substituted for the *definiendum*, there no longer remains any symbol which could be supposed to represent a class. Thus classes, so far as we introduce them, are merely symbolic or linguistic conveniences, not genuine objects as their members are if they are individuals. . . . In the case of descriptions it was possible to *prove* that they are incomplete symbols. In the case of classes, we do not know of any equally definite proof. . . . It is not necessary for our purposes, however, to assert dogmatically that there are no such things as classes. It is only necessary for us to show that the incomplete symbols which we introduce as representatives of classes yield all the propositions for the sake of which classes might be thought essential.

This introduces considerable confusion. First, Russell speaks of classes as being incomplete symbols when he must surely have meant to say that class-symbols were such; for classes, not being symbols at all, cannot be incomplete ones.

This is no doubt merely a slip and can be easily rectified. But, much more seriously, Russell is now writing as though to show that X is an incomplete symbol is tantamount to showing that there are no Xs; thus he does not claim to have proved that classes (or class-symbols) are incomplete symbols because he cannot prove that classes do not exist. But Russell had at the most shown that descriptive expressions were logically eliminable from propositions, as in the case of classes; by eliminating the descriptive expression 'the master of Plato' from a proposition one does not show that the master of Plato does not, or did not, exist.

What happened to cause this confusion, we may reasonably conjecture, is this. Notwithstanding general epistemological considerations of a common-sense kind, Russell, as we have seen, at one time thought that logical considerations demanded that one should admit that the round square and other equally queer entities had some sort of being. The analysis of descriptions freed him from this logical argument and enabled him to say quite freely that there were no such things as round squares. But he now spoke of himself as having proved that definite descriptions were incomplete symbols which stood for no 'genuine objects' when he should rather have said that the analysis of descriptions had abolished an apparent proof of the existence of objects designated by any and every description, so that one was left to decide on the merits of each case whether a descriptive phrase stood for anything or not. Similarly, when he spoke of there being no equally cogent proof that classes were incomplete symbols he should rather have said that there were not objections of a general character to admitting classes as genuine objects equally cogent with those against admitting some objects apparently denoted by descriptions. At this stage at least Russell was prepared to admit that all class-symbols denoted classes as genuine objects, though he doubted it; but he was not willing to admit that every descriptive phrase denoted an object; but he misrepresented the matter to make it appear that to say of an expression that it was incomplete was inevitably to suggest that it did not stand for any genuine object, though this was in no way implied by the original definition of incomplete symbol.

Thus for a time Russell could think of his logical analysis as a metaphysically powerful weapon which enabled him to get down to the basic realities, whereas in fact it merely enabled him to see the mistake in certain logical arguments for admitting as basic entities things which he was rightly reluctant so to regard. Owing to this confusion the expression 'incomplete symbol' acquired a meaning, going beyond Russell's official definition, which it was never to lose, a meaning which included the implication not merely that such a symbol was theoretically superfluous but that there was no basic reality for which it stood. Because of the official definition one could still perhaps say in a mild logical mood that 'the master of Plato' or even 'the red sense-datum' was an incomplete symbol, without denying that Plato had a master or that sense-data were basic entities. But when one said in a more metaphysical context that 'the average man' or 'the class of vertebrates' was an incomplete symbol there was a clear implication that the average man and the class of vertebrates were not basic constituents of the world.

Thus Russell's original contribution to the problem obscured rather than clarified the need for two types of analysis if atomism is to be upheld, the logical type which will improve the form of our statements and the more metaphysical type which will enable us to get some way at least on the way back to basic facts and distinguish these from others. We had better turn to the somewhat clearer accounts of the matter which later emerged.

It will be as well to make our new approach to the subject by means of a sketch of certain doctrines in the theory of knowledge put forward by Russell. In his article entitled

'Knowledge by Acquaintance and Knowledge by Description', which was originally published in 1911 (reprinted in *Mysticism and Logic*), he had maintained that when we make a judgement all the elements in the judgement must be such as are actually present to the mind at that time, with which we are at that time acquainted; for all thought requires the presence of its object before the mind. Thus, given direct sense-awareness of something red, we can judge 'this is red', where *this* is a logically proper name, because both the particular which is a constituent of the fact and its redness, the component of the fact, are directly present to us. But a problem is presented by judgements about things which can never be objects of acquaintance, such as the average Englishman or, according to the sense-datum theory, even physical objects. There is even a problem about things with which we can be or have been acquainted, when we are not actually aware of them, such as our last sense-datum but one. The fact, or the elements in it, cannot be before the mind in such cases, and Russell did not wish to postulate a special entity, the proposition, as the object of thought. Russell's answer to this problem was to say that the things themselves are in such cases not elements in or objects of our judgement. Let us suppose that the judgement has the verbal form 'Caesar crossed the Rubicon'; let us also take it that we are not now directly acquainted with Caesar or with the Rubicon—Caesar is dead and we are not standing on the banks of the Rubicon. Here Russell would claim that neither Caesar nor the Rubicon themselves can be elements in our judgement, and hence the terms 'Caesar' and 'Rubicon' must be functioning as descriptions rather than as proper names. To be logically adequate the sentence 'Caesar crossed the Rubicon' must be rephrased first as 'the man whose name was Caesar crossed the river whose name is Rubicon' to make it clear that it is descriptions with which we are dealing, and then, to eliminate the descriptions, as 'there is one and only one x and one and only one y such that x was named Caesar and y is named Rubicon, and x crossed y'. Now in the case of characters and relations, which are universals, once acquainted is always acquainted, and in our proposition as reformulated we have no particulars mentioned except the words 'Caesar' and 'Rubicon', with which we are acquainted as we produce them, but only universals; it is a general proposition about the relations of certain universals. So we are able to make the judgement at the expense of referring only indirectly to the fact that Caesar crossed the Rubicon by means of a general proposition. Judgement, Russell held, is a special multiple relation between the thinker and all these components. The fundamental point is that 'Every proposition which we can understand must be composed wholly of constituents with which we are acquainted'.[1]

Now this theory incidentally explains to some extent the demand that in atomic propositions all the elements shall be names of constituents of the atomic fact; for otherwise we do not directly indicate or picture the fact but only pick it out indirectly by means of a general proposition. But there is another point of the utmost importance contained in germ in the theory, which plays a great part in the theory of logical atomism and of analysis. There is, it appeared, all the difference in the world between propositions which contain descriptions when the objects described might have been named in suitable circumstances, and those in which the descriptive phrases could not possibly be replaced by proper names. The latter require a much more thorough-going analysis.

An illustration will help to elucidate this point. Let us consider first a proposition in which descriptions are employed but in which the use of logically proper names is in principle possible. We may assume that 'Caesar crossed the Rubicon' is such a proposition for the purposes of illustration, in other words, we may assume that, as Russell claimed,

[1] *Mysticism and Logic*, p. 219.

'Caesar' and 'Rubicon' are really descriptions, but that these descriptions are of objects which are genuine particulars, and which, therefore, could be named under suitable conditions. Then, if we had been at the right place at the right time we might have said 'This crosses that', producing an atomic proposition which pictured an atomic fact. Thus we have here undoubtedly an atomic fact of the form aRb. The fault of the version 'Caesar crossed the Rubicon' is that it looks like the atomic proposition which pictures this fact whereas it is really a general proposition that picks out the fact only in an indirect way. It is a general proposition masquerading as an atomic one; thus the grammatical form of the proposition is misleading with regard to the logical form, but the fact which it purports to picture is there to be pictured.

But contrast a case where the proposition contains descriptive elements, concealed or explicit, which could never even in theory be replaced by proper names, since the descriptions are of things with which we could not conceivably be acquainted. Consider, for example, the propositions 'The average man has an i.q. of 60' and 'The unicorn is a ferocious beast'. Now it is to be presumed that neither the average man nor the unicorn is the sort of thing with which we might be directly acquainted, to which one could give the logically proper name 'this'; we could normally call the average man an abstraction and the unicorn fictitious. Nor, in a mood of robust common sense are we willing to regard the average man and the unicorn as inferred entities, inaccessible, but part of the basic contents of the universe, so that they could have proper names used of them if only they were accessible. This kind of proposition is thus more radically misleading than, for illustrative purposes, we took 'Caesar crossed the Rubicon' to be. For the latter misleads only by purporting to picture a fact when it only refers indirectly to one, being a general proposition. This misleadingness can be eliminated by the sole means of the technique which the theory of descriptions provides. But our propositions about the average man and the unicorn, even if we take them to be true, have a more serious defect; for they not only purport by their grammar to picture atomic facts when, logically, they are general propositions, but also they suggest that there is a single atomic fact to be pictured when in fact the reference is to a multiplicity of facts. Hence we have here a double deceit. If we compare the case of 'Caesar crossed the Rubicon' to simple impersonation of a real man, then here we have impersonation when there is nobody to impersonate. To pretend that one is what one is not is a single fraud, as when one impersonates the Queen of England. But to impersonate the King of France would be a double fraud, both suggesting that one is what one is not and suggesting that there is a person who does not in fact exist. We may also recall that, in Wittgenstein's words 'any one [fact] can either be the case or not be the case, and everything else remain the same'; but we do not believe that the i.q. of the average man could remain the same however ours varied, nor that unicorns can be fierce independently of the activities of myth-makers.

Now it is obvious to anyone whether he be an analyst or not that to say that the average man has an i.q. of 60 is a compressed way of saying that the quotient of the sum of all men's i.q.s divided by the sum of men is 60, and that statements about unicorns can in some contexts be regarded as compendious statements about myths. Let us now see what use the analysts made of such illustrations as these.

First, they introduced a narrower use of the expression 'incomplete symbol' than that which, as we have seen, Russell officially gave. In her book, *A Modern Introduction to Logic*, Miss Stebbing, relying on unpublished work of G. E. Moore, offered the following explanation:

We may perhaps say that 'S' in a given usage is an incomplete symbol when 'S' occurs in an expression expressing a proposition and 'S' is neither a name nor a descriptive phrase referring to a particular which is a *constituent* of the proposition through some property belonging to the particular. . . . Mr. Russell's account of incomplete symbols suggests that he simply meant to distinguish incomplete symbols from names, but, as Professor Moore has pointed out, this account does not fit in with Mr. Russell's practice; it is in the sense distinguished by Professor Moore that the notion of an incomplete symbol is required in order to define what is meant by a 'logical construction'.

Similarly Wisdom offered the short explanation of the term that a phrase is said to be an incomplete symbol if it is one which neither names nor describes what might have been named. This is clearly a narrowing down of Russell's official usage, for according to him any descriptive phrase was an incomplete symbol.

In the light of this account of incomplete symbols the expression 'logical construction', introduced rather casually by Russell, was given a technical meaning. If 'X' is an incomplete symbol then Xs are logical constructions. Thus if the expression 'the average man' is an incomplete symbol we may say that the average man is a logical construction. Let us now suppose that 'Y' is either a name or a description of something which could be named, then Xs are logical constructions out of Ys if and only if for every sentence containing the incomplete symbol 'X' an equivalent sentence can be found containing the symbol 'Y' but not the symbol 'X'; or we can say that if Xs are logical constructions out of Ys then every statement about Xs can be replaced by one equivalent to it which says something, but not the same thing, about Ys. Thus, since 'the average man' is an expression which neither names nor describes what can be named, 'the average man' is an incomplete symbol, and hence the average man is a logical construction. Now let us suppose that ordinary men are genuine particulars and not logical constructions; then we may say that the average man is a logical construction out of ordinary men, meaning thereby that for any sentence about the average man (containing the incomplete symbol 'the average man') an equivalent sentence can be found saying something but not the same thing about ordinary men (containing names of men but with a different continuation to the sentence). That the rest of the sentence will be different, that we shall not say the same thing about the logical construction and that out of which it is constructed, is in general obvious. Thus if we say that the average married couple has 2·345 children, the equivalent statement about ordinary married couples which we hope to find will not attribute this number of children to any of them.

Except perhaps for Russell, who was often careless about words when not concerned directly with formal logic, it was common form among analysts to insist on the following points about this technical vocabulary:

(1) The expression 'logical construction', being defined in terms of 'incomplete symbol', is so used that to say that Xs are logical constructions is to utter a verbal proposition, i.e. a proposition about words. For to say that Xs are logical constructions is, by definition, a way of saying that the expression 'X' is neither a logically proper name nor a description of the nameable. Thus Miss Stebbing could say: 'To say that tables are logical constructions is not to say that tables are fictitious, or imaginary, or in any way unreal. It is, as we have seen, to say something about the way in which we must use the word 'tables' in any expression expressing a proposition about tables.' In slightly later times this point might have been put into the technical language of Carnap's *Logical Syntax of Language* by saying that 'Xs are logical constructions' is in the material mode of speech. But we must note that, having made the statements just quoted on page 158 of her *Modern Introduction to Logic*, Miss Stebbing goes on to say on page 502: 'It is difficult to give clear examples of logical constructions, for the assertion that, for example, *this table is a logical construction* is a metaphysical statement. To

accept the statement is to accept a certain metaphysical analysis.' It is clear that the contention that talk about logical constructions is about language will require further investigation. Russell himself, who sometimes spoke of logical fictions instead of logical constructions, seems to have had his doubts about it.

(2) As a corollary of the first point it was considered to be wholly improper to say such things as 'I am writing on a logical construction', even if one holds that tables are logical constructions. This was thought to involve a confusion of types, somewhat like saying that since men are numerous Socrates must also be numerous.

(3) Further, to say that something is a logical construction is not to say that it is in any way fictitious; the unicorn happens to be both a logical construction and fictitious, but the average man is a logical construction and not a fiction. (This is very like Berkeley's claim that he did not deny the reality of apples.)

(4) To say that something is a logical construction is not to say that it is a mental construct like one of Locke's complex ideas. A logical construction may be psychologically basic. Those who said, for example, that tables were logical constructions out of sense-data did not wish to imply that in the way of experience we start with sense-data and group them into tables.

It may be of help to remark here parenthetically that apart from purely illustrative examples like the average man the most popular candidates for the status of logical constructions were such things as physical objects out of sense-data (phenomenalism), states out of their members, persons out of the sort of thing Hume said that they were bundles of (for the 'bundle' language of Berkeley and Hume is a crude version of the terminology of logical constructions), classes, series, numbers, and the other things which have always given empiricists considerable discomfort and thus have fallen victims to

Occam's razor. Russell, indeed, rephrased the traditional formula *Entia non sunt multiplicanda praeter necessitatem* to read 'Wherever possible replace inferred entities by logical constructions', inferred entities being those which cannot ever be objects of acquaintance.

The elimination of logical constructions, carried out by replacing in propositions all incomplete symbols by names of possible objects of acquaintance, is then another sort of analysis. It was variously called new-level (as opposed to same-level), or philosophical (as opposed to logical), or directional, or reductive, analysis. Different names were patronized by different analysts—usually a new name was chosen to indicate some theoretical refinement in the account given of the nature of this sort of analysis; but it is beyond our compass to deal with such minutiae. We shall normally speak of new-level analysis, since it seeks to get down to the basic facts, and contrast it with the same-level analysis which merely improves the form of statement without change of level.

It will help to bring out the difference between same- and new-level analysis if we give even a rudimentary example. Russell's theory of descriptions will serve again. It will be remembered that he gave as an analysis of 'The A is B' something which may be roughly paraphrased as 'There is one and only one thing which is both A and B'. This was intended to bring out the logical form of the proposition, concealed as it was behind a misleading grammatical form. But it makes no difference whether we substitute for 'The A is B' such a proposition as 'My present visual sense-datum is red' or such as 'The modern age is materialistic'. The first is transformed by same-level analysis into something like 'There is one and only one thing which is a visual sense-datum for me now and it is red'; the other becomes 'There is one and only one thing which is a modern age and it is materialistic'. Yet in the first case, we may suppose, the fact indirectly indicated could be pictured by some such a sentence as 'This is red', for we are dealing with an object of acquaintance; but in the second case, it is equally reasonable to suppose, we are dealing with a most rarified logical construction. Here same-level analysis has left us with an assertion that there is an entity characterizable as being a modern age, and this could hardly be an object of acquaintance. The metaphysical problem with which we are thus left would have to be dealt with by means of a new-level analysis. As a first step in new-level analysis we might transform 'The modern age is materialistic' into something like 'There are many people now living who have materialistic beliefs, and there are few or no people now living who have not materialistic beliefs'. This step would eliminate only the incomplete symbol 'the modern age'; further new-level analysis would be required to get rid of such an incomplete symbol as 'materialistic beliefs'. We can here only illustrate the principle of new-level analysis; we cannot give an example which would be fully worked out.

Thus same-level analysis involves only logical and not metaphysical progress, though it may be an indispensable preliminary to such progress. That is why it was sometimes called logical as opposed to philosophical or metaphysical analysis. It solved logical puzzles rather than giving metaphysical insight. It did not eliminate logical constructions. But if metaphysics is 'a study of the ultimate nature of reality' as McTaggart had said in *Some Dogmas of Religion*, then new-level analysis, even if, as claimed, its method is verbal, is surely metaphysics, for it aims at the achievement of 'a clearer insight into the ultimate structure of facts' as Wisdom claimed in *Mind*, 1935, p. 195. One is here, to use now Russell's words, 'getting down to the ultimate simples, out of which the world is built, simples having a kind of reality not belonging to anything else'. It is clear, too, that the linguistic correlate of this increasing metaphysical insight is an approach nearer and nearer to the ideal language which contains nothing but explicit truth-functions of atomic propositions, each picturing one atomic fact. If the structure of reality is, ideally at least, pictured by the structure of language, the metaphysics of atomism follows from the practice of new-level analysis in the medium of an extensional language. This analysis is necessary because, as Wittgenstein said, ordinary language disguises the thought, and hence we generate bogus problems about the nature of reality, so that 'most propositions and questions, that have been written about philosophical matters, are not false, but senseless'. In an ideal language reality would be pictured and no puzzles would be generated. To this end same-level analysis corrects our syntax, new-level analysis abolishes the misleading simplicity of ordinary talk by replacing logical constructions by basic realities, by eliminating incomplete symbols. The method of philosophy is thus linguistic, though the aim is insight and the abolition of puzzles.

B. ANALYSIS AND THE METAPHYSICS OF ATOMISM

If asked to justify the use of these two methods of analysis, their exponents would first of all have pointed to the practice of all philosophers in history. Plato's analysis of negation in terms of otherness is an example of same-level analysis. The treatment by the British empiricists of the problem of the external world is an example of new-level analysis, even if the technique be crude. Plato's Socrates wished to analyse statements about courage, piety, and justice, Hume to analyse statements about causes. In so far as one thinks one has achieved a correct analysis one feels that one has made philosophical progress.

If it be granted then that this view of analysis is in general sound, why should we accept the metaphysics of logical atomism? If the auxiliary theses of the extensional character of language, and the identity of structure of language, or at any rate an ideal language, and fact, be granted, then in a loose sense we may say that the metaphysics of atomism is thereby implied. But no one, probably, wished to claim that the metaphysical position of atomism could be rigidly proved. But if we wish to understand why people came to adopt the metaphysics of logical atomism, it is not difficult to give a general explanation, though naturally such a general explanation cannot be expected to explain all the details.

Metaphysicians of very different intellectual habits have recognized that a metaphysical system, a view of the general nature of reality, must be built up from the directly known. The rationalist Descartes was willing to start only from the indubitable, the clearly and distinctly perceived; Locke, Berkeley, and Hume had also tried to give an account of things starting from the ideas which they took to be the basic given. Even the extreme rationalist McTaggart started from the empirical fact that something exists, and tried to prove everything from that. Now some of these philosophers were prepared to infer from the given to other, non-given, entities as extra items. They inferred the existence of such things as God, substance, universals, the ego, which they did not claim to be non-inferentially discoverable. Those who see no harm in going that way will not accept logical atomism. But many philosophers, and not only modern logical atomists, have felt that there was something quite bogus about inferred entities. Remember the scorn which Berkeley poured upon poor Hylas's attempt to get beyond ideas to a material substance; remember Hume's insistence that all our ideas are copies of antecedent impressions; remember the difficulties which nearly all philosophers have found in the causal and representative theories of perception as involving such transcendental inferences. Particular inferences to something not given here and now need not cause much trouble; like Berkeley, we can use science to infer from the occurrence of one given idea to the future occurrence of another; if the new idea does occur, the inference was correct, otherwise it was mistaken. But the philosophers' inferences to extra entities which are never given can be neither confirmed nor rebutted in this way, they are idle and uncontrolled. Common sense usually reacts in this way in simpler cases; only a limited number of philosophers, and no men in the street, have wished to hold that because there are the words, nouns, 'redness' and 'equinity' there were therefore separate entities, redness and equinity, or that England was an entity over and above Englishmen, or thought that the world was populated by an infinite host of timelessly subsistent propositions, including self-contradictory ones; though it must be admitted that common sense has not always taken this line in more subtle cases.

But it is not nonsense to say that Euclid's propositions are eternal truths, or that England expects every man to do his duty, or that we are the same people as we were yesterday, even if there be, in a metaphysical sense, no such objects as propositions, states, and egos. We must, therefore, in such cases be talking in an elliptical manner about some real entities; this is the point made by saying that we are talking about the things out of which the proposition, the state, the ego, are logical constructions. So far, then, logical atomism is putting in a general way the metaphysical implications of the practice of empiricist and other tough-minded metaphysicians throughout the ages, just as the technical account of new-level analysis is only an account in an exact and explicit form of the procedure used by Berkeley in his account of the physical world, and Hume in his discussion of causation. Thus we satisfy the metaphysicians desire that everything should be founded in the given, and at the same time avoid the scandal of inferred entities, by showing that in a way we never, except in appearance, go beyond the given.

As for the thesis of extensionality, in its metaphysical employment, that clause of it which maintains that all atomic propositions are logically independent of each other, and that any might be changed, all others remaining the same, might well be regarded as a new, generalized, and more explicit version of Hume's doctrine that all our perceptions are independent existences; and the clause which maintains that all complex propositions are truth-functions of atomic propositions might be regarded as a sharpened form of the doctrine that all our complex ideas are built up out of simple ideas. So we may regard the metaphysics of logical atomism not, as may have appeared from our first bald account of it, as a sudden dogmatic bolt from the blue, but as an effort to think out with entire generality, clarity, and consistency the presuppositions and implications of empiricist practice and outlook throughout the ages, with the aid of the new logical tools available.

4

INTERIM REVIEW OF LOGICAL ATOMISM

THE latter part of the discussion in Chapter 3 arose from the need to answer two questions which we had set ourselves. They were concerned with two imagined objections which we allowed to interrupt the account of logical atomism in which we were engaged. The questions we asked were concerning the relation of atomism to our professed subject, philosophical analysis, and secondly concerning the justification for accepting the metaphysics of logical atomism. It has become clear that these questions are by no means unconnected. On the one hand, we may attempt to justify logical atomism as a statement of the metaphysical implications of the analytical practices of empiricist philosophers throughout philosophical history; conversely the metaphysics may be regarded as showing the point of, and thus justifying, the practice of analysis. It is abundantly clear that the acceptance of the metaphysics of logical atomism demands the practice of analysis, for the most striking evidence in its favour would be a continued success in the production of analyses of the kind which it claims to be theoretically possible. But we must not think that these empiricist considerations were the only ones operative; the influence of theorizing about mathematics was as strong here as it was with Descartes. The truth-functional logic had been originally devised as a tool for the logical investigation of mathematics; even the theory of descriptions and the theory of logical constructions were in the first instance tools for this purpose. Given a belief that logic was the skeleton of language, with the variables marking gaps for constants, it was easy to think that the success of the logic as a tool in investigating mathematics justified a belief that it was the skeleton of an adequate language; what could adequacy be but identity of structure? It is the more important to bear this aspect in mind as it will be comparatively little discussed by us. We are mainly concerned with the relation of atomism to analysis; from this angle the best argument available in defence of atomism was the rhetorical question: if the aim of new-level analysis is not to get back to the basic, ground-floor facts, what is it? At this stage no alternative hypothesis was forthcoming, though we shall see that later analysts, who rejected logical atomism, tried to provide one. That analysis was a correct philosophical method, no one doubted, even though it was desirable to give it a theoretical rationale.

We started with a crude outline of logical atomism. We have now completed a second, somewhat more finished, sketch of this view, together with an indication of its relation to the practice of analysis. But still we have only an outline, in which we have, moreover, been carefully avoiding questions whose difficulty demands a more thorough study. Our next main task will be to examine some of these difficult points. It might be asked whether this threefold method is really necessary, why there could not have been a single careful discussion. The twofold answer is, firstly that the discussion of any one part of the subject in detail before its connexions with other elements of the view were known would have seemed impossibly obscure and pointless; secondly, it is worth while to try to see the wood as such, before we scrutinize individual trees, and to see it in such a way that we can understand and admire its general appearance before we have to consider any reasons for chopping it down. But before we do proceed to this more detailed examination which is now required, a few general reflections and comments may be helpful.

First we may note that we have here a position which is conservative in so far as it sticks to a quite recognizable version of an old and perfectly respectable view of the task of metaphysics. True, it rejects speculative metaphysics, the metaphysics of inferred entities. But this is not novel. Kant had declared such metaphysics to be impossible. But there are old and respectable definitions of metaphysics as an effort to think clearly and consistently about the world, or as to understand the nature of ultimate reality. This might be called critical as opposed to speculative metaphysics. Bradley was in intention a metaphysician of this kind, for he was asking what the nature of reality must be if it appears to us in the way it does, not seeking to pierce the veil of appearances but to make sense of them; though Russell naturally stressed his opposition to such philosophers as Bradley, the atomists did not think that they were opposing a right conception of metaphysics to a fundamentally different wrong one. They thought that they were opposing a scientific, correct way of doing it, to a slipshod, incorrect method. They were doing the same sort of thing but very much better.

Metaphysics, then, is an investigation of the world, though, in Wisdom's words, it is concerned with acquiring new knowledge of facts, not knowledge of new facts. In general this attitude was shown by an insistence that philosophy was concerned with the analysis of facts, not of propositions, though we do not find complete agreement on this point. Here is a quotation at some length from a document of the period which should help to make clear the traditional element in the attitude of these philosophers to metaphysics. In her article 'The Method of Analysis in Metaphysics', Miss Stebbing said:

Metaphysics is a systematic study concerned to show what is the structure of the facts in the world to which reference is made, with varying degrees of directness, whenever a true statement is made. In so far as the aim of metaphysics were achieved, it would enable us to know what precisely there is in the world. To know what precisely there is in the world is to know what are the facts which together make up, i.e., constitute, the world. To know precisely what a given fact is, is to know both the elements which make up the fact and the mode of their combination. In other words it is to know the structure of the fact. Hence the aim of metaphysics is to reveal the structure of that to which reference is made in true statements. It follows from this view of metaphysics that the metaphysician is not attempting to discover facts of a kind comparable with those studied by any of the natural sciences or with any other distinctive branch of knowledge, such as history. In a sense, the metaphysician is not concerned to discover any *new facts*; he does not add to the sum-total of human knowledge in the way in which the natural scientist or the historian does.

This view that the job of the philosopher was the analysis of facts was, I think, made easier to hold by some widely influential work of G. E. Moore. Moore was never to be included among the logical atomists himself, and he refrained after his earliest period from much speculation about the nature of philosophy; but he had a great influence upon the logical atomists who did so speculate, and worked in close touch with them. Perhaps the most important element in his influence was the scrupulous care and candid confession of difficulties which he showed in his own analytical work and the ruthless scrutiny to which he subjected the slipshod attempts of others; but for the moment we are concerned with a more specific point. In a celebrated short account of his position which he called 'A Defence of Common-Sense', Moore had maintained that there were a great number of common-sense propositions of which he claimed to know the truth without possibility of doubt. The sort of thing which he claimed to know was that he had two hands, was looking at an ink-pot, &c. Having claimed to know the truth of these propositions, Moore went on to admit that he had in most cases no knowledge of the correct analysis of these propositions. This confirmed the analysts in their view that their job was to analyse, not to question, the deliveries of science and of common sense, for Moore had a devastating way with those who denied his common-sense knowledge. But the special interest from our present point of view can be made clear by means of a further quotation from Miss Stebbing's article 'The Method of Analysis in Metaphysics'.

Assumption 2 must be briefly considered. This is equivalent to the assertion that some propositions can be known to be true. I do not suggest that directional analysis is impossible in the case of false propositions. Such a suggestion would be absurd since we often do not *know* what we assert is true or false, and sometimes we are led to reject a possible view because the directional analysis of a proposition shows that something would have to be the case which we do not believe to be the case. But I do wish to assert that those who have used the method have made the assumption and that the assumption is reasonable.

Unless *we can know* that some certain proposition is true, i.e. asserts a fact, the analysis of that proposition will not enable us to *know* anything about the constitution of the world. I do not pretend to be able to justify the assumption, but it seems to me to be plausible. Nor do I know any conclusive reason against it. . . . If there is *no* proposition which we can know to be true, then there is no metaphysical method capable of yielding knowledge.

We could, if we liked, put Miss Stebbing's point by saying that the translation of sentences can only be analysis of facts if the sentence expresses a fact. And, if metaphysics is analysis of facts, we could never know whether we were doing metaphysics if we did not ever know that we were on this occasion dealing with a true proposition. Some, including Wisdom and probably Wittgenstein, would not have liked Miss Stebbing's statement that one can directionally analyse a false proposition. In such cases they would have said that one was analysing a possible fact and so getting knowledge of reality. Wittgenstein said 'The picture [i.e. the proposition] displays a possible state of affairs in logical space'. Wisdom put it this way: 'Of course it is possible to give a philosophical analysis of a false proposition *S is P*; but this is to say what would be the analysis of the fact which the sentence 'S is P' would locate if it did locate a fact.' Wisdom hated the word 'proposition', which he thought was a very misleading incomplete symbol indeed. Moore's vindication of common-sense knowledge gave some secure material for metaphysical investigation.

So much for the traditional, backward-looking element in the analytic position. But there was another forward-looking element. For we have observed that the source of metaphysical puzzlement was traced, not to the complicated or elusive nature of reality, but to the misleading nature of conventional language. Thus philosophical problems are in a way linguistic problems. There would be no need for philosophy if language were not inadequate. Again, we must remember that such statements as that X is a logical construction have to be interpreted as linguistic statements; 'X is a logical construction' = ' "X" is an incomplete symbol'. Further analysis consists in the translation of statements; in itself it is a linguistic procedure. In a comparison between analysis and translation in the ordinary, non-philosophical sense (and his remarks would apply to paraphrase within a single language with a non-philosophical purpose), Wisdom said:[1] 'The distinction between translation and analysis is not a distinction between what is said, but between why it is said.' In other words, the only non-linguistic thing about philosophy is its aim of revealing the structure of the facts.

In saying that these elements were forward-looking, we must not be taken to mean that they are all novel in the history of philosophy. They are rather the elements which were to have an important sequel. Nor must we over-estimate the linguistic side of things at this stage. For we have seen that the purpose of the linguistic moves was metaphysical, and it was also the case that the test of adequacy of analysis was not linguistic, but rather some metaphysical insight. Furthermore,

[1] *Mind*, 1933, p. 195.

these two elements, the traditional metaphysics and the assertion that philosophical statements are the product of linguistic confusion, are not easy bedfellows. Wittgenstein had simply produced a metaphysics and had said: 'My propositions are elucidatory . . . he who understands me finally recognizes them as senseless.' For he was too impartial not to mete the same treatment to himself as to others. Other philosophers who had claimed that philosophical error was due to linguistic error, such as Spinoza, had usually considered that they were exempt from this confusion, that there were philosophical problems and statements which did not arise from linguistic confusion. It is clear that this impartial spirit, admirable in its way, has its difficulties for a philosopher. Though it was to be of great importance later, this side of Wittgenstein was regarded by most British philosophers for a time as an eccentricity to be disregarded. We shall temporarily disregard it also.

We must just note at this stage that this forward-looking element makes it hard to see to what extent we are dealing with an empiricist position. The question is itself vague, for the notion of empiricism is an obscure one. We can safely say that for the thorough-going radical upholder of this position all the basic propositions were intended to be empirical ones, and the basic facts were therefore usually taken to be facts of sense-experience. It was partly because Wittgenstein held this view and considered that his metaphysical statements could not be reduced to empirical statements that he was unwilling to exempt them from the charge of being products of the abuse of language. Most of the atomists, however, took the line of compromise in demanding that the propositions they discussed should be empirical without demanding that the propositions in which they discussed them should be empirical also. There was, moreover, a difficulty whether the basic propositions which were to be dealt with were in fact empirically given. They often appeared more in the guise of theoretically postulated entities, of which one could never be certain that one had found one. The fact behind this apparent inconsistency is that the majority of atomists had not fully realized and were unprepared to admit the more radical implications of the doctrine that all atomic propositions are empirical.

The case of ethics furnishes us with a good example. Most of the atomists had been fully indoctrinated by Moore, and did not believe that ethical propositions were capable of a naturalistic interpretation, or in other words did not believe that ethical propositions could be regarded as truth-functions of atomic empirical propositions. Hence the consistent Wittgenstein said:[1] 'There can be no ethical propositions. Propositions cannot express anything higher. It is clear that ethics cannot be expressed. Ethics is transcendental.' But not all the analysts could stomach this. Moore, the least influenced of all by metaphysical, empiricist considerations, simply held that there were ultimate ethical facts. Not all the atomists could stomach this either. In fact most of them studiously avoided ethics at this period. We must not regard them as deliberately burking an issue; but they certainly did not face it.

In general then it seems true to say that the atomists were empiricists in so far as the sort of thing that analysts suspected of being logical constructions were those things which cannot be seen, heard, touched, &c., and that they tried to analyse them in terms of things that could. If empiricism, however, can only be ascribed to those who operate not only on, but also with, empirical propositions and tautologies exclusively, then it is clear that the atomists were not empiricists. Most of them in fact insisted that they were constructing a metaphysical position. This clearly leads to an internal strain, to the view that the propositions of logical atomism are senseless. Wittgenstein himself, we have seen, accepted this and said that his propositions were nonsense. Most did not at this stage

[1] *Tractatus*, 6.42.

see so far. It might be claimed that one can still carry out the procedures of analysis if one accepts Wittgenstein's position; on the ground that to say 'p is equivalent to q' where p is the analysis and q the analysandum is to utter a tautology if true, and tautologies are not nonsensical. But the old rationale of analysis—logical atomism—can only be produced, as Wittgenstein recognized, by violating one's own rules for talking sense.

Thus the logical atomists were mostly inconsistent empiricists in two ways; they did not recognize the implications of their general position for such fields as ethics, and they had a doctrine of what were possible statements which excluded the doctrine itself. It was essential for them either to stop being empiricists and to recognize with Moore that there were atomic ethical facts, and presumably metaphysical facts such as 'This is an atomic fact', or else to find a rationale for their analysis other than logical atomism, and, moreover, one of a non-metaphysical character. We shall find them realizing this in due course.

In these general remarks we have had cause to notice again and again that from the strict empiricist principles which the atomists often enunciated it would seem to follow that their metaphysics was devoid of meaning; for it could hardly be construed as empirical in content. But this is no reason why we ourselves should dismiss logical atomism out of hand and without further examination. For it is not necessary for us to agree that only empirical statements are significant, and there is a great deal in the metaphysics of atomism which is worthy of further investigation. We must, therefore, now examine in some detail some of the more important aspects of logical atomism against the background of the general account of the position already given, and therefore without danger of losing perspective or of failing to see the wider significance of these comparatively detailed questions.

5

FACTS AND PICTURES OF FACTS

IN this chapter three of the most important and characteristic doctrines of logical atomism have been selected for treatment in comparative detail. First the relation between facts and their ingredients is discussed, then the question of what different types of fact could be admitted on atomistic principles, and finally the relation of language and the world, or picture of fact and fact.

A. THE BASIC DATA: FACTS AND THEIR INGREDIENTS

In discussing the relation between facts and their ingredients we shall in effect be discussing the nature of what the logical atomist takes to be the basic data or ultimate realities at which in theory we finally arrive by process of analysis.

The first problem which we must consider is this: we have at times talked in terms of the reduction of all propositions to atomic, or basic, propositions, and at times we have talked of the reduction of things, regarded as logical constructions, to the most basic things, the nameable particulars. Are we then to say that the basic elements are things or facts? The consideration of this problem required some subtle metaphysics from the atomists, who were not agreed on the answer to it.

Russell regarded the basic elements as particulars. Thus he says in his articles on logical atomism:[1]

The reason that I call my doctrine *logical* atomism is because the atoms that I wish to arrive at as the sort of last residue in analysis are logical atoms and not physical atoms. Some of them

[1] *Monist*, 1918.

will be what I call 'particulars'—such things as little patches of colour or sounds, momentary things—and some of them will be predicates or relations and so on.

So we see that although most of Russell's analysis is carried out in terms of atomic facts, it is the constituents and components of these which are the ultimately basic data. An atomic fact for Russell is a fact in which all the constituents and components are independent, self-subsistent, logical atoms, and which is not complex by way of containing such logical constants as *or* and *if-then*. This is a single requirement, in so far as a fact must be complex ultimately, if not in appearance, if its constituents are not logical atoms.

Most atomists would probably have accepted the intermediate position adopted by Wisdom in his discussion of the relation of things, facts, and events in the second of his articles in *Mind* on logical constructions, to which the reader is referred. Wisdom summed up this position as follows: 'An account of the world in terms of things, an account of the world in terms of facts, and an account of the world in terms of events is just an account of the world in three languages.' One could, for example, on this view, indifferently enumerate a number of red sense-data, or a number of facts that *this* and *that* (where *this* and *that* are logically proper names of sense-data) are red, or say that so many reddings are occurring (on the analogy of the German *es grünt*).

But some atomists, including Wittgenstein, preferred the language of facts, for very metaphysical reasons, which we must now consider. We shall do so with reference to Wittgenstein's famous statements in the *Tractatus*, which have often been imperfectly understood. Here are some selected quotations from the first few pages of that book, with the authors marginal numbering:

1   The world is everything that is the case.
1.1 The world is the totality of facts, not of things.

1.11   The world is determined by the facts and by these being all the facts.

1.2   The world divides into facts.

2   What is the case, the fact, is the existence (Bestehen) of atomic facts.

2.01   An atomic fact is a combination of objects (entities, things).

2.011   It is essential to a thing that it can be a constituent part of an atomic fact.

2.012   In logic nothing is accidental: if a thing *can* occur in an atomic fact the possibility of that atomic fact must already be prejudged in the thing.

2.0121   . . . Just as we cannot think of spatial objects at all outside space, or temporal objects outside time, so we cannot think of any object apart from the possibility of its connexion with other things.

If I can think of an object in the context of an atomic fact, I cannot think of it at all apart from the *possibility* of this context.

2.0122   The thing is independent, in so far as it can occur in all *possible* circumstances, but this form of independence is a form of connexion with the atomic fact, a form of dependence . . .

2.0124   If all objects are given, then thereby are all possible atomic facts given also.

2.013   Every thing is, as it were, in a space of possible atomic facts. I can think of this space as empty, but not of the thing without the space.

2.02   The object is simple.

2.021   Objects form the substance of the world. Therefore they cannot be compound.

2.0231   The substance of the world can determine only a form and not any material properties. For these are first presented by the propositions—first formed by the configuration of the objects.

2.032   In passing; objects are colourless.

2.024   Substance is what exists independently of what is the case.

2.0272   The configuration of objects forms the atomic fact.

We must now elucidate these somewhat Heracleitan utterances.

It is clear that we are now at a much deeper metaphysical level than we were when we considered Russell's statement that particulars were such things as small coloured patches. (This is not to imply that Russell was unaware of these deeper problems.) Let us suppose that we have a small red patch. Already we have an empirical contingent fact that it (whatever it is) is red; it might have been green. Thus, though it must be the sort of thing which can be green or red or blue, having the colour cannot be essential to its nature. In Wittgenstein's epigrammatic style we can put these points by saying that while the possibility of any atomic fact (such as it being red) must already be prejudged in the thing (2.012), none the less, considered in themselves, objects are colourless (2.032); with the colour you get a fact. Particulars in this more basic sense must be things capable of being Russell's sort of particular, but when you have Russell's sort of particular you have already a fact.

We are now dealing with the notion of substance. Wittgenstein said that objects form the substance of the world, and it would seem that Wittgenstein's objects are very like the Aristotelian first substance as it appears in the *Categories*. We cannot go into the difficulties of scholarship which surround the interpretation of Aristotle, but we may consider briefly what he says. Aristotle here groups the predicates which may be asserted of a subject term under a number of headings, each group being called a category; thus under the category of quality fall such predicates as 'red' or 'wise' or 'sweet'; under the category of relation fall such predicates as 'bigger than that' or 'next to that', and so on. But these predicates must be predicated of a subject, and some subjects are first substances, things of which any predicate in any of the other categories may be predicated and which can themselves be predicated of nothing. In a way, then, substance must be prior to its possible predicates, it must be separable in thought from them in order that it may have them affirmed of it. It is not a red thing, for example, but that of which the quality *red* may be predicated; the thing which may be black or red or green. The Aristotelian first substance might also be said to be colourless. Now every student of Aristotle's *Categories* points out that this first substance is apparently a very difficult logical abstraction, hard to think of as independent and prior to all else. This is what Wittgenstein seems to be pointing out when he says that objects cannot be thought of except in the context of a possible atomic fact. He denies that the basic, independent realities out of which the world is composed can be such as these, and makes his basic elements in the world facts. Clearly he does not deny that something like an Aristotelian first substance has to be thought of as a distinguishable feature of facts, but not as a separable feature—a fact is not just a collection of elements. Take an atomic fact pictured by 'This is red'; then 'this' names the object. We can think of it outside the context of this particular fact, for we can think of it as being brown or blue or . . .; but we cannot think of it except as being red or brown or blue or . . . . That is to say, we cannot think of it outside all atomic facts. But, again, the type of object determines what facts it can logically enter into. One sort can enter into such facts as 'This is loud' or 'This is shrill', but not into such facts as 'This is red'. And the same, of course, applies vice versa. 'This' and 'that' are logically proper names of things which can be thus or thus, not of things which are thus and thus. Otherwise 'This is red' would be a tautology; as is easily seen by taking the word 'this' to stand for the small red patch of which Russell speaks. We would be contradicting ourselves if we said it was brown; but we must be able to continue to use the same name of the particular if 'brown' be substituted for 'red'.

It should be clear now that Wittgenstein took a particular

to be the kind of thing that Aristotle called a first substance, but denied, as students of Aristotle might well agree to be plausible, that such a thing was more than an abstraction. Aristotle might well have agreed that such an object cannot exist without the attributes predicated in the other categories, and this is very similar to saying that objects cannot exist outside facts. If this explanation has had any success it will now be seen why Wittgenstein took the fact as the basic entity. It is, so to speak, the only kind of basic entity that can be found which is self-subsistent, and not merely an abstraction. The difficulty which many find in interpreting the non-symbolic parts of the *Tractatus* is very largely due to the fact that they do not realize how thoroughly metaphysical it is.

The reader might now wish to read again the quotations from the *Tractatus* which we have been discussing. For the sake of those who do some detailed comments on the more obscure apophthegms are here added.

2.011   This is like saying that it is essential to the Aristotelian first substance that it can have attributes.

2.012   Thus a noise as such may be shrill, but not red, &c.

2.0122   The thing is dependent in that its nature is wholly determined by the range of facts into which it can enter.

2.013   We can think, for example, of there being nothing red, but not of a thing which is not possibly red, or at least possibly of some sort—in some logical space.

2.021   If objects were not simple they might be dissolved into elements which would be the real substance.

2.0231   What objects there are determines what can be the case, but not what actually is the case. If a red patch were an object, then its existence would determine that something was the case—that something was red.

2.032   This is a way of saying that objects are what can be red, &c., not what is already of one of these colours.

So much for the reasons for starting with facts rather than

with things. It must, however, be clear that Wittgenstein and Russell do not really disagree here, since the object which Wittgenstein rejects as independent reality is something much more rarified than Russell's particular, which already comprises facts in Wittgenstein's view. There could be a great deal more discussion of this matter, but the scale of our enterprise demands that we turn to other questions about the basic elements. We will in future talk of these basic elements as facts on the Wittgenstein model.

B. TYPES OF FACTS

Granted, then, that it is facts and not things to which we have to work back in analysis, and which are the logically basic and irreducible elements, we must now learn what types of irreducible facts there are. In this part of the discussion we shall always mean such basic irreducible facts when we speak of facts, unless it be otherwise indicated. There was some disagreement on how many kinds of fact there were; as Russell recognized an unusually liberal variety of facts, we may start by going through those he recognized, indicating where others denied that a type recognized by Russell was in fact a separate basic type.

(1) *Atomic facts*

First, then, Russell recognized the particular atomic fact which is the kind of fact which we have been considering with regard to Wittgenstein. This is the sort of fact in which there is one component (character or relation) and n constituents. There is, for example, the fact with one component and one constituent, such as *this being red*, *that being shrill*, and so on, subject-attribute facts which we can symbolize ϕa or $R(a)$. This is the monadic fact. The a stands for some object, something like the Aristotelian first substance as we have seen. Russell and most of the atomists thought of them as being sense-data, more short-lived than Aristotle's substances, though this is not an essential part of the metaphysics but rather a result of the longing for the indubitable starting-point, which so many of them shared with Descartes, combined with the sense-datum theory of perception.

In addition to subject-attribute facts, there are facts with one component and two constituents. These are facts where the component is a dyadic relation, *this being on that, that being greater than this*, and so on. They can be symbolized *aRb*, or, to preserve similarity of form, $R(a,b)$. We may also have triadic facts such as *A giving B to C*, which is symbolized $R(a, b, c)$. There are also facts with four terms to the relation, such as *Jones sending a letter to Smith by post*, to be symbolized $R(a, b, c, d)$, and generally *n*-adic facts of the form $R(a, b, c, \ldots n)$. Whether there are any facts with a given degree of complexity cannot be known *a priori*; at best we can know *a priori* that such facts are possible. 'How', asked Wittgenstein, 'could we decide *a priori* whether I can get into a situation in which I need to symbolise something with the sign of a 27-termed relation?'

This, then, is one kind of fact, the particular fact, as Russell called it, or the atomic fact. We might as well say here that this was the only kind of fact recognized by all analysts, and a consistent logical atomism would forbid the recognition of others. It was the paradigm of facts, such that the most hard-headed could recognize it. Other kinds of fact were not recognized by the thorough-going, and everyone forgot them when they possibly could. This is why no mention was made of other kinds of fact in our general sketch of atomism.

But Russell recognized other kinds of fact. We shall now in turn consider the other kinds of fact which he recognized, giving his reasons for recognizing them and indicating the means by which other people tried to escape recognizing them. As a rough generalization we may say that no one ever suggested that there were any more sorts of fact beyond those which Russell recognized as a matter of general theory, though they did from time to time and in special contexts allege there to be facts which are hard to fit into even Russell's comparatively liberal classification.

(2) *General facts*

One type of fact recognized by Russell in addition to particular facts is the general fact. In Lecture V of the *Monist* articles, to which the reader is referred for further details of his discussion, he says: 'It is clear I think that you must admit general facts as distinct from and over and above particular facts.' We must examine Russell's reasons for making this admission, for it is an admission. He certainly was not motivated by any affection for general facts, especially so far as facts of the form 'All *A* is *B*' are concerned, though he says: 'Of course, it is not so difficult to admit what I might call existence-facts—such facts as "There are men", "There are sheep", and so on. Those, I think, you will readily admit as separate and distinct over and above the atomic facts I spoke of before.' Why Russell considered that there was this difference in acceptability between these two sorts of general fact is very hard to divine, and all the more so since in his logic existential propositions and universal propositions are defined as being equivalent; thus *all A is B* is defined as equivalent to *it is not the case that some A's are not B*. However, Russell accepted both universal and existential facts, and the gist of the argument for them was as follows. Consider first a proposition which is traditionally called completely enumerative—'All the *A*s are *B*'. Now, Russell argues, one might think that this was just a summary statement of a number of particular facts—*this is A and B, that is A and B*, and so on through all the *A*s. But however tempting this may be at first sight, it would be a mistake. For the proposition 'All the *A*s are *B*' tells us something more than these particular facts, namely, that these are all the *A*s. And this is clearly a general fact. The case becomes still more favourable to general facts if we take the non-enumerative universal proposition of traditional logic—'All *A*s are *B*'. Here again a mere enumeration of particular propositions will not take the place of the original, partly for the reasons which applied to the enumerative proposition, and partly because this proposition does not make an assertion about a closed, enumerable class, such as all the books on this shelf, but about an open class, a class of indefinite extent, such as the class of all books. But you cannot write out in detail the members of an indefinitely large class, and hence you cannot write a list of particular propositions about them. So, as such propositions as 'All men are mortal' clearly tell us facts in some sense, and as we see that we cannot analyse these facts into sets of atomic facts, we are driven to recognize such general facts as a special kind of irreducible fact. Thus we see that the guiding principle of Russell's argument is that when a proposition cannot be analysed into a truth-functional complex of atomic propositions it must be recognized as stating a special kind of fact of its own. This is clearly a very reasonable type of argument.

It is not difficult to see why atomists were unwilling to accept this contention of Russell's. It considerably detracts from the beauty and simplicity of the metaphysics, and general facts did not seem to be as hard and acceptable as particular facts. The fact of this cat being on the mat, or eating fish, seems to be given to the beholder, it is there to see, but such a fact as all cats being carnivorous is a much more abstract affair. We must therefore examine some alternatives to Russell's view.

It will be useful first to consider shortly some points about the logical behaviour of general propositions. It is tempting to regard them as follows: the universal proposition we analyse by treating, for example, 'Everything is *A*' as an infinite conjunction of singular propositions 'This is *A* and that is A and . . .'; similarly we analyse the existential proposition 'Something is (or some things are) A' as an infinite disjunction of singular propositions 'This is A or that is A or . . .'. Thus there seems to be an analogy between the universal proposition and the truth-functional conjunction, and between the existential proposition and the truth-functional disjunction. Some analysts who did not like to admit that there were general facts claimed that there was an identity, not merely an analogy. But it is hard to see how such a view can be made acceptable, for it completely fails to take any account of Russell's arguments which we have just noticed, and it is in any case distinctly odd to speak of an infinite conjunction or disjunction as though it was just a special case of conjunction or disjunction. None the less it does perhaps shed some light on general propositions to look at them in this way. And perhaps there is more to say for this point of view than has been recognized here. For Wittgenstein argued in its favour, and Ramsey said in his paper 'Facts and Propositions':[1] 'About these [i.e. general propositions] I adopt the view of Mr. Wittgenstein that "For all x, fx" is to be regarded as equivalent to the logical product of all the values of "fx", i.e. to the combination fx_1 and fx_2 and fx_3 and . . ., and that "There is an x such that fx" is similarly their logical sum.' Thus Ramsey is in agreement with Wittgenstein, and it is very unwise to say of such gifted philosophers that their views are silly, even if they may be wrong. But in fact they never appear to have answered Russell's arguments. However, we shall soon see that Ramsey himself came to reject this view (as, it appears, Wittgenstein did too), so even the promoters of the view evidently came to see flaws in it.

We cannot omit reference to another view about general propositions which was developed in its most complete form by Wisdom in his articles on logical constructions. It required a very complicated technique for exact statement, so

[1] *The Foundations of Mathematics*, p. 152.

we must be content with indicating its general character in our own words. Wisdom's basic thought was that though it was impossible to maintain that general propositions had the same meaning as, could be analysed in terms of, a conjunction or a disjunction of particular propositions, none the less this did not imply that they stated a special kind of fact. The facts to which they referred were the same, but the general propositions referred to them in a different, less explicit manner. The facts which justified a general proposition such as 'All *A*s are *B*' were particular facts such as *this A being B*, and similarly the facts which falsified them were also particular facts. But the particular facts are not pictured by the general proposition, as they would be by a conjunction or a disjunction. Rather as a green patch on a map refers to a set of trees, and not to anything over and above them, though it does so inexplicitly by not mapping them individually, so the general proposition indicated a range of particular facts without explicitly stating them. The general proposition thus neither depicted a new sort of fact, nor did it have a defect of level by picturing a construction out of atomic facts as though it were an atomic fact, but simply a defect of explicitness in its reference to atomic facts. Thus 'I met a man', which by Russell's theory of descriptions is a general proposition, differs from 'I met Jones' not by asserting a different sort of fact but by failing to make quite clear what fact it is asserting.

But the most interesting and radical attempt to deal with the problem is to be found in Ramsey's second thoughts on the subject in his paper 'General Propositions and Causality'. Though this paper was never finally prepared for publication, and contains special difficulties on that account, we find in it a brilliant summary of the position. Referring to propositions like 'Arsenic is poisonous' and 'All men are mortal', he asks:

Why are these not conjunctions? Let us put it this way first: What have they in common with conjunctions and in what way do they differ from them? Roughly we can say that when we look at them subjectively they differ altogether, but when we look at them objectively, i.e. at the conditions of their truth and falsity, they appear to be the same.

$(x).\phi x$ differs from a conjunction because

(a) It cannot be written out as one.

(b) Its constitution as a conjunction is never used; we never use it in class-thinking except in its application to a finite class, i.e. we use only the applicative rule. [Ramsey is here rejecting his earlier view that it could be treated as a logical product on the ground that in argument we do not treat it as such—e.g., to accept a law in science is not like accepting a very long conjunction.]

(c) It always goes beyond what we want to know, or can; cf. Mill on 'All men are mortal' and 'The Duke of Wellington is mortal'. [This, as Ramsey realises, is much the same point as (b). The reference is to the chapter 'The Use and Value of the Syllogism' in Mill's *System of Logic*.]

(d) The relevant degree of certainty is the certainty of the individual case, or of a finite set of individual cases; not of an infinite number which we never use, and of which we couldn't be certain at all.

$(x).\phi x$ resembles a conjunction

(a) In that it contains all lesser, i.e. here all finite, conjunctions, and appears as a sort of infinite product.

(b) When we ask what would make it true, we inevitably answer that it is true if and only if every x is ϕ; i.e., when we regard it as a proposition capable of the two cases truth and falsity, we are forced to make it a conjunction, and to have a theory of conjunctions which we cannot express for lack of symbolic power. . . .

If then it is not a conjunction, it is not a proposition at all, and then the question arises in what way it can be right or wrong.

This superb specimen of *a priori* metaphysics with which he follows up his brilliant statement of the problem is most worthy of note: 'If then it is not a conjunction it is not a proposition at all.' Here is a counter-attack with a vengeance! Russell had said in effect: 'We cannot treat general propositions as simple truth-functions, conjunctions, therefore we must admit general facts.' Ramsey in effect replies: 'Since the only facts are particular facts, atomic facts, and since all propositions are statements of atomic fact, or reducible to such, and since general propositions are not reducible to such, therefore they are not genuine propositions at all.'

But to show that from this point of view Ramsey has produced a piece of *a priori* metaphysics is not to show that he has said something silly or valueless. Like any good metaphysician Ramsey has given good intelligible arguments for his position. It is good metaphysics to say that general propositions do not state facts in the way that singular propositions do. Ramsey develops his position by claiming that it is an artificial way to look at general propositions to think of them as true or false; the question is not whether we are to accept a general proposition or its contradictory, i.e. whether it is true or false, but rather whether we are to adopt it or to do without it. We ask: 'Do we accept this as a law?'; and here the true alternative to accepting the law is simply to do without it.

But if Ramsey is to maintain that such utterances as 'Arsenic is poisonous' are not to be construed as propositions, he must put an alternative construction upon them. The exact interpretation of Ramsey's unrevised paper, which he would never have published in the form we have it, is not easy. But he appears to hold that such verbal forms must be regarded as rules which we may or may not adopt for guiding our expectations, and from which we can derive singular propositions; thus 'Arsenic is poisonous' is a rule that one should treat anything which is arsenic as poisonous, and given a sample of arsenic we can frame the singular proposition 'If this is arsenic, it will be poisonous' in accordance with the rule. A general belief, Ramsey held, consists in the acceptance of a rule and a habit of singular belief. Thus he sought to escape between the horns of the dilemma, on one horn of which Russell, on the other Wittgenstein, seemed to be impaled. We shall find that a view very like Ramsey's was to find favour with some of the logical positivists, though they also supported it with arguments drawn from quite different considerations.

Here the problem of generality must be left. It is no part of the plan of this book to attempt to arbitrate in these debates, or to work on the problem of generality for its own sake. Our plan is to exhibit the reasons why generality was a problem for the analysts and to relate some typical ways in which they tackled the problem, which never ceased to exercise them; enough has perhaps been said for the achievement of this limited aim.

(3) *Negative facts*

The problem of generality was discussed at this particular point because we had observed that Russell recognized general as well as particular facts in the course of our consideration of the kinds of fact recognized by the atomists. But this was not the only heterodoxy of Russell's. Russell also recognized negative facts. But it must not be thought that he recognized these as a third sort of fact alongside particular and general facts. It is rather that Russell recognized four sorts of fact, particular positive, particular negative, general positive, and general negative. The distinction 'positive-negative' has a different *fundamentum divisionis* from the distinction 'particular-general'.

Russell introduced these negative facts in Lecture III of his *Monist* articles in this charming way:

Are there negative facts? Are there such facts as you might call the fact that 'Socrates is not alive'? I have assumed in all that I have said hitherto that there are negative facts, that for example if you say 'Socrates is alive' there is corresponding to that proposition in the real world the fact that Socrates is not alive. One has a certain repugnance to negative facts, the same sort of feeling that makes you wish not to have a fact '*p* or *q*' going about the world. You have a feeling that there are only positive facts, and that negative propositions have somehow or other got to be expressions of positive facts. When I was lecturing on this subject at Harvard I argued that there were negative facts, and it nearly produced a riot: the class would not hear of there being negative facts at all. I am still inclined to think that there are. . . . It is a difficult question. I really only ask that you should not dogmatise. I do not say positively that there are, but there may be.

It is important to note the matter-of-fact tone of all this; it is as if one were asking whether there are mice in the kitchen. At these lectures Russell was asked: 'Would the existence of negative facts ever be anything more than a mere definition', and he answered: 'Yes, I think it would. It seems to me that the business of metaphysics is to describe the world, and it is in my opinion a real definite question whether in a complete description of the world you would have to mention negative facts or not.'

Though we should take the atomists seriously, it is irresistible to give at this point a rather comic illustration of the matter-of-fact way in which Russell at this period conceived metaphysics. The articles by Russell in the *Monist* are in the form of lectures and report even the questions asked at the end of the lectures and Russell's replies to them. At the end of one lecture the following dialogue occurs:

Q. If the proper name of a thing, a *this*, varies from instant to instant, how is it possible to make any argument?
Mr. Russell: You can keep 'this' going for about a minute or two. I made that dot and talked about it for some little time. I mean it varies often. If you argue quickly, you can get some little way before it is finished. I think things last for a finite time, a matter of some seconds or minutes or whatever it may happen to be. [Lecture II.]

It is in this matter-of-fact way that Russell asked whether there were any negative facts.

Russell's reasons for accepting negative facts are not far to seek. He accepts a correspondence theory of truth. If

'Socrates is alive' is false, it is so because it is out of correspondence with the facts. But with what fact in particular is it out of correspondence? It must be the fact that Socrates is not alive. If there were no such fact, what would be wrong with 'Socrates is alive'? Russell did consider one much-canvassed alternative view, that 'not-p' means the same as 'There is some proposition q which is true and incompatible with (or excludes) p'. For example, on this theory the proposition 'This piece of paper is not red' means the same as 'There is some true proposition which is incompatible with "This paper is red"'. The true proposition in question is no doubt the proposition that it is white, but the theory is not so absurd as to claim that 'This is white' is a part of the meaning of 'This is not red'. It only claims that a part of the meaning of 'This is red' is the assertion that there is some true proposition incompatible with 'This is red' without saying which. But Russell rejects this view on the ground that it makes a complex fact of incompatibility between propositions, one unspecified, a basic sort of fact, and this is objectionable on three counts: (i) because incompatibility is no less metaphysically disturbing than the simple negative as a basic element in facts, (ii) because this theory makes a complex fact basic—'p being incompatible with q', (iii) because elements in the alleged fact are propositions, and Russell did not consider propositions to be capable of being basic elements; they are logical constructions. It is clear that it would have to be propositions and not facts between which the incompatibility held, for facts could not be logically incompatible with each other; for them we should have a logically impossible world.

We are told by Russell that Harvard nearly rioted at the suggestion of negative facts; it may be safely added that they were no more popular in analytic circles. But, as we found with the problem of generality, there was no ready-made alternative. Wisdom, writing twelve years later, said:[1]

[1] 'Logical Constructions', *Mind*, 1931, p. 469.

We have dealt with 'This is red', but what about 'This is not red'? Does it sketch a fact? Does *not* name an element in the world? I shall not try to answer that question here. I shall not decide whether 'This is not red' sketches a fact. I dodge the difficulty by saying that it negatively sketches a fact. This just means that its positive, viz. 'This is red', does sketch a fact.

If this is all that Wisdom would say in a series of articles in which he attempted to give a precise answer to every other problem about the nature of analysis, we may reasonably conclude that the analysts had developed no satisfactory answer to Russell. Ramsey, however, had as usual an interesting contribution to make to the problem.[1] He pointed out that it was hard to think that 'not' named some element in a fact, such as the relation of incompatibility; for it is only an accident of our symbolism that we have the word 'not' at all. We might, he pointed out, express negation not by inserting the word 'not' but by writing what we negate upside down. Secondly, it is to be remembered, Ramsey said, that p is equivalent to the double negation not-not-p. Thus if we wrote negative statements upside down, double negation would consist of turning it right way up again. But if 'not' named an element, then a double negation ought to name that element twice. Thus the incompatibility theory would lead us to interpret 'not-not-p' on the lines of 'Some proposition is true which is incompatible with the proposition that a proposition is true which is incompatible with p'. Ramsey's own solution, which was not widely accepted, was in terms of positive attitudes of belief and disbelief, so that to assert 'not-p' is to assert a disbelief in p.

Once again, we cannot pursue the problem of negation throughout all its ramifications, but it should now be clear in what way and why it was a problem and the kind of way in which people set out to tackle it. If 'not' did not name an

[1] *Foundations of Mathematics*, pp. 146 ff.

element in the world, it must be eliminable, and it did not seem to name an element in the world; but the analysts were never really satisfied that they had found a way of eliminating it. Of course, any correspondence theory of truth is faced with this sort of problem, but the picturing theory was a very fundamentalist version of the correspondence theory. As we shall see later, the analysts had a particular reason for accepting this fundamentalist position.

(4) *Facts corresponding to intensional functions*

We may note in passing, though it is much too specialized a matter for us to examine in detail, one other odd kind of fact which Russell felt himself reluctantly compelled to recognize. We have seen that it was a generally accepted tenet of the atomists that language was truth-functional, that the connexions between propositions were purely extensional so that the truth and falsehood of complex propositions could be determined solely from the truth and falsehood of the elementary propositions of which they were composed. In general Russell accepted this thesis; but he could not see his way to deny that there were some complex propositions which were not thus truth-functional, and these he called intensional functions. If we take, for example, the statement '*A* believes that *p*', we have, or so it appears, a complex proposition *p* as a proper part or element. According to the thesis of extensionality, if *p* is an element in the complex proposition then the truth or falsity of the complex proposition will be in part determined by the truth or falsity of *p*. But if '*p*' is here an element in the complex proposition '*A* believes that *p*' a difficulty arises. For '*A* believes that *p*' is clearly not a truth-function of '*p*', since its truth in no way depends on the truth of '*p*'. It is what was called in *Principia Mathematica* an intensional function. So the extensional thesis is endangered. Partly with this consideration in mind, though other factors influenced him, Russell flirted with the behaviourist doctrine that 'A believes that p' is to be analysed as saying that A behaves in such and such a way, so that not the proposition 'p' but the words 'p' would be elements in the fact. In the *Analysis of Mind* Russell accepted this doctrine; in the *Monist* articles he rejected it. It is important to remember that, at least in Russell's case, the desire to save the truth-functional interpretation of language was one factor, and quite an important one, in leading to the analysis of belief in terms of behaviour.

Here, too, there was no consensus of opinion among the analysts on the method of dealing with this difficulty. Wisdom dealt with it, as he dealt with negation, by a sort of conjuring trick. For example, when speaking of atomic facts he says:[1] 'I use atomic because I think I mean by "atomic" what Russell and others have meant by it. But they have said that atomic facts cannot contain other facts. My atomic facts can. E.g. *I observe that this adjoins that* contains *This adjoins that*.' He says also:[2] 'I do not say that all compound sentences are logical constructions out of simple sentences. I am inclined to think "He fell because he laughed" is not. I think "because" names a relation. . . . Whether "p entails q" can be dealt with I do not at present decide.' Perhaps it is unfair to call this a conjuring trick. But when atomic facts are allowed to contain other facts the old metaphysical rigour of the position has gone, while the words remain the same.

We cannot go further now into this problem of 'intensional functions'. We must be content to see it as a running sore for the upholders of the view that language has the logical skeleton of a truth-functional logic; a full discussion would involve both a radical examination of this general thesis and a close examination of the sort of statement which caused these special difficulties. That lies beyond our present scope.

[1] 'Logical Constructions', *Mind*, 1933, p. 55, note.
[2] Op. cit., *Mind*, 1931, p. 471, note.

C. TYPES OF ULTIMATE FACTS—SUMMARY

It is clear that the ideal picture which all the atomists had before them was a world consisting of only the particular atomic facts, all other candidates for the role of ultimate fact being somehow reducible to these. Wittgenstein rigidly maintained this view, which is clearly the purest form of logical atomism. Others admitted extra kinds of fact with extreme reluctance when faced with propositions of a kind which appeared to resist all attempts at analysis of the required pattern; but this admission was made with the proviso that work must go on at this sort of difficulty in the hope that such propositions would be found after all to be amenable to truth-functional analysis. Doing this work was the form which the problem of negation, the problem of generality, &c., took at this period for these philosophers. We might here use the language of theology and say that it was a pious belief that the general, the negative, the intensional, &c., fact could be analysed away; but it could not be *de fide*.

What was *de fide* was first that most of the ostensible particular facts of everyday talk could be analysed in terms of other facts which were genuinely atomic. Facts about states, for example, were regarded as certainly thus analysable; perhaps only facts about sense-data were not thus analysable, and everything else was logical constructions. Secondly, it was *de fide* that in 'the actual objective world' there were, in Russell's words, no facts 'going about which you could describe as "*p* or *q*" '; generally, there were no molecular facts. No one could have serious doubts on these points and be called an atomist.

We have said that no one could doubt these basic articles of faith and be called an atomist. And yet Russell was not only the high priest, he was the arch-heretic. At one point in the *Monist* articles he said:

There is one point about whether there are molecular facts.

I think I mentioned, when I was saying that I did not think there were disjunctive facts, that a certain difficulty does arise in regard to general facts. Take 'All men are mortal'. That means: ' "x is a man" implies "x is mortal" whatever x may be.' You can see at once that it is a hypothetical proposition. It does not imply that there are any men, nor who are men, and who are not; it simply says that if you have anything which is a man, that thing is mortal. . . . It comes down to this that ' "x is a man" implies "x is mortal" is always true' is a fact. It is perhaps a little difficult to see how that can be true if one is going to say that ' "Socrates is a man" implies "Socrates is mortal" ' is not itself a fact, which is what I suggested when I was discussing disjunctive facts. I do not feel sure that you could not get round that difficulty. I only suggest it as a point which should be considered when one is denying that there are molecular facts, since, if it cannot be got round, we shall have to admit molecular facts.

So Russell; but he was notoriously not a reliable party man. In general one did not suggest that there might be molecular facts, for that would be the end of logical atomism. To be more serious, it is a wonderful and admirable thing about Russell how candidly and exhaustively he would raise difficulties about the views he had fathered. His distaste for infanticide could never prevail against his hatred of error.

This concludes our discussion of the types of fact admitted by the atomists in the classical period of analysis. The significance of this discussion for analysis is not far to seek; for the correlate of the metaphysical doctrine 'there are such and such sorts of fact, and no other' is the rule of analysis that a satisfactory final analysis will contain only clauses of a certain sort—those which could be held to be pictures of these sorts of fact.

D. PICTURES OF FACTS

Wittgenstein, in the *Tractatus*, started with an account of facts and objects which finishes at 2.063. The next statement is 2.1—'We make to ourselves pictures of fact.' We cannot do better than follow this order of discussion, so we shall turn to consider the doctrine of the analysts regarding the relation of language to fact, of which the central thesis is the doctrine of picturing. By no means all the atomists used the terminology of 'picturing' or agreed with the detailed views of those who did. But, if extreme, the doctrine of picturing was very influential and was in a way typical; so we shall consider it rather than other less characteristic versions. The most important documents are *Tractatus* 2.1–3, 3.1–3.2, and 4.01–4.02; and Wisdom's 'Logical Constructions, I', *Mind*, 1931, pp. 201 ff.

First a terminological point. We have so far used the word 'proposition', which Russell customarily used, in our account of atomism. The word also appears in the English translation of the *Tractatus*; but the German word here is *Satz*, which is the ordinary German for 'sentence'. When Wittgenstein says (3.1) 'In the Satz the thought is expressed perceptibly through the senses', it would seem that 'sentence' is an appropriate translation. Wisdom certainly took the picture to be a sentence. We shall therefore speak of sentences in this section, modifying the translation of Wittgenstein accordingly. For 'sentence' makes it a little clearer than 'proposition' would how Wittgenstein could think of the picture as a physical fact, even if it remains odd to call a sentence a fact rather than a thing.

But in saying that the doctrine was that sentences, as pictures, were physical *facts* we are not simply being careless; for it was regarded as an important logical insight that the picture is not a thing but a fact. Words are things; a jumble (*Gemisch*) of words would be nothing more than a collection of things. But a sentence, Wittgenstein emphasized, is not merely a jumble of words; it is a complex of words with an internal structure, when considered as a vehicle of thought. Just why this particular sort of complex is a fact can perhaps best be made clear in the form of a commentary on some of the most obscure dicta in the whole of the *Tractatus*.

The passage for comment is this:

3.14 The sentential sign consists in the fact that its elements, the words, are related to one another in it in a definite way. The sentential sign is a fact.

3.141 The sentence is not a jumble of words (just as the musical theme is not a jumble of notes). The sentence is articulated.

3.143 That the sentential sign is a fact is concealed by the ordinary form of expression, written or printed. (For in the printed sentence, for example, the sign for a proposition does not appear essentially different from a word. Thus it was possible for Frege to call the sentence a composite name.)

3.1431 The essential nature of the sentential sign becomes very clear when we imagine it compounded of spatial objects (such as tables, chairs, books) instead of written signs. The mutual spatial position of these things then expresses the sense of the sentence.

3.1432 We must not say 'The complex sign "*aRb*" says "*a* stands in relation *R* to *b*" '; but we must say, '*That* "*a*" stands in a certain relation to "*b*" says *that aRb*'.

In this passage the most obscure utterances are unfortunately the ones numbered 3.1431 and 3.1432, which are intended to explain the others. It is on them that we must concentrate. 3.14 states the doctrine that the sentential sign is a fact. 3.141 and 3.143 state that while it appears to be of the same nature as a word, except in so far as it may seem to be a mere collection of words, merely longer than a word, this appearance is due to a defect in our form of expression. Frege had spoken without discrimination of the sense (*Sinn*) and reference (*Bedeutung*) of both words and sentences,[1] and Russell had said in Lecture I of his *Monist* articles which were written prior to the publication of the *Tractatus*:

It is very important to realise such things, for instance, as that

---

[1] e.g. *Frege Translations*, ed. Black and Geach, p. 62.

propositions are not names for facts. It is quite obvious as soon as it is pointed out to you, but as a matter of fact I had never realised it until it was pointed out to me by a former pupil of mine, Wittgenstein. It is perfectly evident as soon as you think of it, that a proposition is not the name of a fact, from the mere circumstance that there are two propositions corresponding to each fact. Suppose that it is a fact that Socrates is dead. You have two propositions: 'Socrates is dead' and 'Socrates is not dead'. And these two propositions corresponding to the same fact, there is one fact in the world which makes one true and one false. That is not accidental, and illustrates how the relation of proposition to fact is a totally different one from the relation of name to thing named.

Wittgenstein was not, then, tilting at windmills.

Now let us consider 3.1431: 'The essential nature of the sentential sign becomes very clear when we imagine it compounded of spatial objects (such as tables, chairs, books) instead of written signs. The mutual spatial position of these things then expresses the sense of the sentence.' The difficulty of this lies in its excessive brevity. It becomes clear by comparison with Wisdom[1] who makes the same point in essentials at greater length. The gist of Wisdom's discussion is this. Let F be the sentential sign which we have to show to be properly a fact, and let the fact to be expressed be F'. Let the fact F' be the (alleged) fact that Wisdom has killed Al Capone. Now let us first use a glass to name Wisdom, a dish to name Al Capone, and symbolize killing with a knife. Then we may put the glass on the knife and the knife on the dish to express F'—Wisdom has killed Al Capone. But this has the same defects as written language. For the knife and the dish and the glass may still look like a mere collection of things, not essentially different from the single thing which serves as a name; equally important is the defect that the knife is the same sort of thing as the glass and the dish—we might perhaps have symbolized Wisdom by a knife and killing by a

[1] 'Logical Constructions, I', *Mind*, 1931, pp. 208–9.

glass. But if we now put the glass (Wisdom) straight on the dish (Al Capone), and symbolize the relation of killing by the spatial relation (*on*) in which the things stand, the matter becomes much clearer. Now we cannot recognize the meaning of the sentence consisting of glass-on-dish without realizing that we are here not dealing with a mere collection of objects, and we no longer inappropriately symbolize things and the relation between them in the same manner. The glass being on the dish is a very different thing from the philosophical tragedy of the dish being on the glass. It is this superior type of symbolization that Wittgenstein recommends in 3.1431, though it must be admitted that through the greater part of his work he speaks as though he were contenting himself with more ordinary methods.

Now the meaning of the statement in 3.1432 which at first sight is so very perplexing becomes clear. We have: 'We must not say "The complex sign '*aRb*' says '*a* stands in relation *R* to *b*' "; but we must say, "*That* '*a*' stands in a certain relation to '*b*' says *that aRb*".' Let *that aRb* be the fact *that Wisdom has killed Al Capone*; then Wittgenstein is saying: 'We must not say "The complex sign 'glass-on-dish' says 'Wisdom has killed Al Capone'"; but we must say "*That* the glass is on the dish says *that Wisdom has killed Al Capone*".' *That the glass is on the dish* is a fact; *that Wisdom has killed Al Capone* is another. Thus one fact states another, by means of its internal structure. The relation of the picturing fact, the sentence, to the pictured fact, the relation of picturing, depends, according to all our authorities, on the identity of structure of the two facts. The structure of language is a clue to the structure of reality. But only a fact, it seemed, could be identical in structure with another fact. If we do not raise fundamental difficulties about the notion of the structure of a fact, which would be out of place at present, this is surely a clear and consistent doctrine.

Language then can be used to express facts, to make

statements, because there are linguistic structures, sentences, the which are facts and which have a common structure with facts to be expressed. We must now consider how this identity of structure was conceived and on what grounds it was claimed. The identity of structure was called 'picturing' and our discussion will proceed by an examination of this notion.

At some stage we shall have to come to grips with the question whether all sentences picture facts, including the sentences of our ordinary language, or whether only the sentences of a perfect language would do so, such sentences as the glass being on the dish. And we shall be faced with the problem, if only perfect sentences picture, of deciding how ordinary non-explicit sentences manage to represent reality, in however inadequate a manner. But for the present we shall confine the discussion to the question how a perfect language would picture reality.

What would a perfect sentence be like? (We are, of course, concerned at present only with sentences which are supposed to picture atomic facts, neglecting other kinds of fact if there are any.) There is first the problem whether we can regard a sentence of the glass-on-knife-on-dish variety as being a perfect representation or picture of a fact that Wisdom has killed Al Capone, or whether only the glass-on-dish variety (the physical juxtaposition showing the relation of *killing*) will do. If only the second sort would do we should have to introduce some quite new conventions into written language, and write, say 'This is to the left of that' like this 'This that', where the relation *to the left of* is shown by the physical arrangement of the words. Then 'This is to the right of that' would become 'That this'. 'This is over that' might become 'This That'. 'This is red' might be changed to the mere writing of 'This' in red ink, and so on. Clearly we should get into terrible and perhaps insuperable difficulties this way, especially if we tried to say anything at all complicated.

Wisdom had an ingenious method of dealing with this

problem. He recognized, apparently with Moore's support, what he called 'first derivative' facts. Suppose that it is a fact that this is red. Then the first derivative will be the fact that this is characterized by red, a dyadic fact, with *red* and *this* for constituents and *characterization* as the relational component. Now if we eliminate the objectionable 'is' from 'This is red' and write 'This red', we have a sentence which represents the fact that this is red in the doubtful glass-knife-dish fashion; but it represents the fact that this is characterized by red in the perfect glass-dish fashion; the fact of the juxtaposition of the words 'red' and 'this' shows the fact of the relation of these elements by the relation of characterization. Thus ordinary language, with comparatively minor improvements, perfectly pictures the first derivatives of the facts we normally take it to represent. Provided that the fact is a genuine atomic fact and not one about, say, states, Wisdom allows us to say that the fact is pictured if the first derivative, at least, is correctly represented. Since most of the atomists did so all the time and the rest did so most of the time, we may, like Wisdom, accept these slightly relaxed requirements for a perfect picture.

What then will a picture in a perfect language be like, granted that we adopt this more lenient criterion of a perfect language? Two requirements which were never seriously challenged are the following: (*a*) there should be exactly the same number of words in the sentence as there are elements in the fact (there would of course be one word less than elements if we symbolized in the ideal glass-on-dish way and still counted the component (i.e. character or relation) as an element); (*b*) each word in the sentence should either stand for some quite determinate component or be the proper name of some constituent of the fact. Since we are still not challenging the conception of facts with a countable number of elements, for we are still trying to understand, not to criticize, we need now raise no difficulty about the former of these requirements. About the requirement (*b*) something must be said, and especially about the notion of a logically proper name, for it is a curious and interesting one.

There are obviously two main questions to be answered about proper names. First it must be explained what a logically proper name is and how it differs from an ordinary proper name; secondly, it must be explained why we must use logically proper names in our sentences if we are to produce perfect pictures, and not, for example, descriptions or ordinary proper names. As usual, we shall find, not the most accurate or the most subtle, but the most simple and direct answer to these questions in the writings of Russell. Here is an extended passage from the *Monist*, 1918:

The only kind of word that is theoretically capable of standing for a particular is a *proper name*, and the whole matter of proper names is rather curious.

Proper Name = word for particulars. *Definition.*

I have put that down although, as far as common language goes, it is obviously false. It is true that if you try to think how you are to talk about particulars, you will see that you cannot ever talk about a particular particular except by means of a proper name. You cannot use general words except by way of description. How are we to express in words an atomic proposition? An atomic proposition is one which does mention actual particulars, not merely describe them but actually name them, and you can only name them by means of names. You can see at once for yourself, therefore, that every other part of speech except proper names is obviously quite incapable of standing for a particular. Yet it does seem a little odd if, having made a dot on the blackboard, I call it 'John'. You would be surprised, and yet how are you to know otherwise what it is that I am speaking of. If I say 'The dot that is on the right-hand side is white' that is a proposition. If I say 'This is white' that is quite a different proposition. 'This' will do very well while we are all here and can see it, but if I wanted to talk about it to-morrow it would be convenient to have christened it and called it 'John'. There is no other way in which you can mention it. You cannot really mention *it* itself except by means of a name.

What pass for names in language, like 'Socrates', 'Plato', and so forth, were originally intended to fulfil this function of standing for particulars, and we do accept, in ordinary daily life, as particulars all sorts of things that really are not so. The names that we commonly use, like 'Socrates', are really abbreviations for descriptions; not only that, but what they describe are not particulars but complicated systems of classes or series. A name, in the narrow logical sense of a word whose meaning is a particular, can only be applied to a particular with which the speaker is acquainted, because you cannot name anything you are not acquainted with. You remember, when Adam named the beasts, they came before him one by one, and he became acquainted with them and named them. We are not acquainted with Socrates, and therefore cannot name him. When we use the word 'Socrates', we are really using a description. Our thought may be rendered by some such phrase as, 'The Master of Plato', or 'The philosopher who drank the hemlock', or 'The person whom logicians assert to be mortal', but we certainly do not use the name as a name in the proper sense of the word.

That makes it very difficult to get any instance of a name at all in the proper strict logical sense of the word. The only words one does use as names in the logical sense are words like 'this' or 'that'. One can use 'this' as a name to stand for a particular with which one is acquainted at the moment. We say 'This is white'. If you agree that 'This is white', meaning the *this* that you see, you are using 'this' as a proper name. But if you try to apprehend the proposition that I am expressing when I say 'This is white', you cannot do it. If you mean this piece of chalk as a physical object then you are not using a proper name. It is only when you use 'this' quite strictly, to stand for an actual object of sense, that it is really a proper name. And in that it has a very odd property for a proper name, namely that it seldom means the same thing two moments running and does not mean the same thing to the speaker and to the hearer. It is an *ambiguous* proper name, but it is really a proper name all the same, and it is almost the only thing I can think of that is used properly and logically in the sense that I was talking of for a proper name. The importance of proper names, in the sense of which I am talking, is in the sense of logic, not of daily life.

Thus we see that to the question: What is a logically proper name? the atomists' answer is that it is a word that, to quote Wisdom's summing up of the matter, 'stands for an object with which we are directly acquainted and . . . indicates an object without ascribing characteristics'.[1] The second requirement, that it should indicate an object without ascribing characteristics, is clearly very like what Mill had said of all proper names, that they have denotation without connotation. Russell's view that ordinary proper names did not fulfil this requirement, but were abbreviated descriptions, was not an eccentricity but almost a platitude at this time; thus Frege had said much the same thing in 'On Sense and Reference', taking it that every word had both a sense (approximately, connotation) and a reference (approximately, denotation), and suggesting that the sense of Aristotle might be 'the pupil of Plato and teacher of Alexander the Great'; and even so unlike-thinking a philosopher as Joseph had attacked Mill in his *Introduction to Logic*, claiming that proper names must have connotation or else be useless.

There are a number of reasons why this curious doctrine that ordinary proper names were abbreviated descriptions was accepted; (i) it was not seen how otherwise such a statement as 'Odysseus was crafty' could be intelligible, for it seemed that 'Odysseus' had no denotation, since Odysseus is but a fiction, and would be a mere *flatus vocis* if it had no connotation either; (ii) it was not seen how 'Tully was Cicero' could be informative, as it is and 'Cicero was Cicero' is not, unless the former could be taken as asserting identity of denotation of two names with different connotation; (iii) harking back to Russell's theory of judgement which we have already outlined, it was not seen how we could understand

[1] *Mind*, 1931, p. 211.

'Caesar crossed the Rubicon' when not in Caesar's presence unless 'Caesar' had a sense or connotation. The requirement that a logically proper name should stand for an object of direct acquaintance was an immediate corollary of this third point—if it was well taken a logically proper name could have denotation without connotation only if used in presence of the object named. As a sort of curious sop to Mill it was conceded that ordinary proper names tried to denote without connoting, and so words like 'this' were called logically proper names as doing what ordinary proper names set out unsuccessfully to do. This doctrine of proper names was an important part of the view of language which was the major cause of disaster to logical atomism, and it must not be thought to be of minor importance.

A short postscript will show the slippery nature of the slope on which proper names lay. Russell had rejected ordinary proper names as not fulfilling requirements, but had felt quite happy about 'this' and 'that'. But this golden age was not to last. Said Wisdom:

I have a similar fear about 'this'. If I speak not to myself but to someone else and say 'This is red' I use 'This' as meaning something like 'The thing to which I am pointing'. It is to be hoped that when I talk to myself I use it to mean something. My last sentence is not a joke. I do not mean by it that it is to be hoped that I use 'This' as I use 'something'! Nor that it is to be hoped that I am not always talking nonsense when I begin a sentence with 'This'. It means that it is to be hoped that sometimes there is something such that I am using 'this' as a name for it.[1]

Now for the other question: Why must we have only logically proper names in our sentences in a perfect language? Russell had said 'You cannot really mention *it* itself except by means of a name'. But we can be more precise than that. Firstly, if we have a descriptive phrase (or ordinary proper name) instead of a logically proper name, we have, according

[1] *Mind*, 1931, p. 203.

to the theory of descriptions, a general proposition. But a general proposition cannot picture a particular fact. As Wisdom put it: 'though if I say "The bay beat him" the descriptive phrase may be said to stand for something—viz. the winning horse—yet the relation here expressed by "stand for" . . . involves the . . . phrase "the bay", the quality *bay* and the horse to which the quality applies.' So that the word 'bay' does not refer to the horse directly, but via a characteristic. Secondly, though it is much the same point in different language, according to Russell's theory of judgement we must be acquainted with all the elements of the judgement. But if we use descriptive phrases we are being acquainted with some qualities and relations, not with the actual thing. But if we have only logically proper names in the judgement we shall in judging be actually acquainted with the things about which we are talking, and not with some substitute. That is the aim. We are already aware from Russell that it is impossible to use proper names of things in their absence, so that we can only produce these perfect pictures of things in their presence. This becomes obvious if we say, with some analysts, 'demonstrative symbol' instead of 'logically proper name'; it is clearer that one can only use a demonstrative symbol for a thing in its presence.

A third, and quite separate, reason for the demand for proper names or demonstratives rather than descriptions in perfect sentences is this. It will be remembered that for Wittgenstein the object was to be conceived as being rather like the Aristotelian first substance, as the subject of predicates regarded in abstraction from its predicates. Now if we refer to one of these things by means of a descriptive phrase we are prejudging in it some characteristic; prejudging, because it is logically prior to this characteristic. It is not merely that we do not refer directly to the horse itself in speaking of 'the bay'; it is also that the logical object might not have been bay but some other colour. Thus the use of descriptions to refer to the constituents of basic facts is metaphysically objectionable, as well as logically objectionable.

Here it is necessary to leave the specific topic of proper names. It requires critical examination, which it will receive later, but it should now be sufficiently clear what the doctrine was for us to return to the main topic of picturing, as a contribution to which our present discussion of proper names has occurred.

If then the sentence has exactly the same number of words as the fact has elements, and if each word is either the name of a constituent of the fact, or stands directly for some component, then the sentence may be such as to picture the fact perfectly. 'To the configuration of the simple signs in the sentential sign corresponds the configuration of the objects in the state of affairs.'[1] Now it clearly cannot be held that these pictures are pictures in the specific way that a representative painting is a picture. Wittgenstein said:

At the first glance the sentence—say as it stands printed on paper—does not seem to be a picture of the reality of which it treats. But nor does the musical score appear at first sight to be a picture of the music; nor does our phonetic spelling (letters) seem to be a picture of our spoken language. And yet these sign-languages prove to be pictures—even in the ordinary sense of the word—of what they represent. It is obvious that we perceive a sentence of the form *aRb* as a picture. Here the sign is obviously a likeness of the signified. (4.011–4.012.)

The gramophone record, the musical thought, the score, the waves of sound, all stand to one another in that pictorial internal relation, which holds between language and the world. To all of them the logical structure is common. (4.014.)

In the fact that there is a general rule by which the musician is able to read the symphony out of the score, and there is a rule by which one could reconstruct the symphony from the line on a gramophone record and from this again—by means of the first rule —construct the score, herein lies the internal similarity between

[1] *Tractatus*, 3.21.

these things which at first sight seem to be entirely different. And the rule is the law of projection which projects the symphony into the language of the musical score. It is the rule of translation of this language into the language of the gramophone record. (4.0141.)

From this passage we can learn a great deal about what was meant by 'picturing'. We are told that the relation of a sentence to a fact is similar to the relation of a musical score to a piece of music; that in each case there is a similarity of structure between the terms of the relation; that the similarity of structure lies in the fact that there is a general rule for the construction, or reconstruction, of one from the other. This general rule can be called a law of projection, or, to say the same thing in terms more appropriate to the case of language, a rule of translation. Understanding a language, therefore, is knowing the general rule for reconstructing the facts which fit sentences or for constructing sentences to fit facts, and there is a similarity of structure because it is possible to give such a rule.

But why should this sort of similarity of structure be called 'picturing', 'even in the ordinary sense of the word', as Wittgenstein claimed? This can be explained, perhaps, though it can surely not be justified. Let us suppose first that we have before us a very life-like picture of Napoleon. Given such a picture an appropriate expert could undoubtedly give us a formula, or set of formulae, which would serve as a rule of projection connecting the contours of Napoleon's face with the lines of the drawing. The law of projection would be very different according as the picture was drawn full-face or side-face, but in either case it could be given. But it is also true that we could find some rule of projection, however odd and full of *ad hoc* conditions, according to which any childish drawing of a face would be a perfectly accurate map of Napoleon's face. Given this rule of projection a skilled person would be able to make a perfect replica of Napoleon's face with the aid of the drawing, or to recognize him, or could reproduce the drawing by looking at Napoleon without having seen the drawing. It would, of course, look very different from the ordinary pictures of Napoleon, but then a full-face picture of him would look very different from one drawn side-face. We can therefore claim, as Wittgenstein is looking at things, that our picture is a perfect picture of Napoleon, although with an odd and unusual projection. If we allow this, we can say that even in the case of ordinary pictures it is not the fact that a picture is recognizable at first glance that makes it a good picture, but the fact that the rule of projection has been accurately followed. An easily recognizable picture might be very inexact, and one entirely unrecognizable at first glance might be very exact. Thus if we eliminate the irrelevant question of first-sight recognizability we can make out a plausible case for the exact parallel between the relation of portrait to man, score to symphony, and sentence to fact which Wittgenstein claims.

If we are right in thinking that this interpretation of the views of Wittgenstein is substantially correct, then though we have tried to give it some plausibility it presents great difficulties. The most fundamental and far-reaching must be neglected for the moment, for they involve the fundamental tenets of logical atomism. But two more specific points may be mentioned. Firstly, Wittgenstein was surely wrong in claiming that even perfect sentences were pictures 'even in the ordinary sense of the word'. To say that this is so involves taking accuracy of projection as the criterion for perfection in a representational portrait. But this will not do. However accurately our childish drawing obeyed some discoverable law of projection, we would not say that it was a portrait of Napoleon, good or bad. Further, the painter has not any specific law of projection in mind when he paints a portrait, so that it is hard to say whether he has followed it accurately; whatever his portrait be like we can always find subsequently some projection which it has accurately followed and some which it has not. Moreover, in so far as the painter has some law of projection in mind, we all know that a portrait may be all the truer to life as the result of some deliberate departures from this law of projection. We in fact call things pictures because of a recognizable likeness, not because of fidelity to some unknown rule of projection.

A more serious point is this. If a law of projection is all that we require for similarity of structure, then the fact that we can find a law of projection connecting any drawing with any object reduces the significance of the demand for identity of structure almost to vanishing-point. So the metaphysical content of saying that sentence and fact must have identity of structure becomes trivial. Even if we have correctly interpreted Wittgenstein's official account of picturing, it is surely clear that he in fact read more into the notion, something more like intuitively recognizable similarity of structure, or having a very simple and general law of projection. When he says 'It is obvious that we perceive a sentence of the form *aRb* as a picture. Here the sign is obviously a likeness of the signified', he means more than that some rule can be given for determining the fact which it states. Internal similarity of structure must be more than this.

If then we go to Wittgenstein to learn more about the similarity of structure between reality and sentences on which the relation of picturing depends, we shall officially get a very thwarting answer. We read:

Sentences can represent the whole of reality, but they cannot represent what they must have in common with reality in order to be able to represent it—the logical form. To be able to represent the logical form we should have to be able to put ourselves with the propositions outside logic, that is outside the world. Sentences cannot represent the logical form: this mirrors itself in the sentences. That which mirrors itself in language, language itself cannot represent. That which expresses *itself* in language, *we* cannot express by language. The sentence shows the logical form of reality. It exhibits it. . . . What *can* be shown *cannot* be said.[1]

But Wittgenstein, who cheerfully acknowledges that, by his criteria, most of the *Tractatus* is nonsense (6.54), has a good shot at saying what can be shown and not said time and time again throughout the book. He would probably be prepared to say that a sentence of the form *aRb* shows that in the fact there are two objects with a certain relation between them, in spite of the fact that the concept 'object', thus used, is a metaphysical pseudo-concept (4.1272). But he would admit that this was no use for one who was unable to see what the sentence showed, for it involves an improper use of language.

But there is a special difficulty here, apart from the general impossibility of there being any significant philosophical sentences. It is peculiar to the doctrine of picturing, interpreted as involving a recognizable likeness, as we have suggested Wittgenstein did in practice interpret it. Let us revert to the portrait of Napoleon and imagine someone who looks at it and complains that he cannot see the likeness. It would be ridiculous if the complaint was that the likeness was not drawn in with the eyes and nose, if he demanded that it should be added to the picture, or that a supplementary picture of the likeness of the picture to the original be drawn. Clearly the likeness cannot be represented, at least *in pari materia*. We can but draw pictures of things and the likeness must show itself. I can draw things having a certain structure, but I cannot draw the structure on its own. This is the special difficulty which Wittgenstein finds here. This is why it is especially hard to produce even bogus elucidations of the notion of similarity of structure. For Wittgenstein everything that can be said is a picture, and can only do what a picture can do.

This doctrine of Wittgenstein's that nothing can be said about the relation of language to the facts if pictured was not found universally acceptable among analysts. The Vienna

[1] *Tractatus*, 4.12–4.1212.

group, which rejected the general thesis that there were no genuine philosophical sentences on the ground that statements about language as such could be considered both philosophical and scientific, none the less accepted this more specific restriction, on the whole, so that Carnap wrote his *Logical Syntax of Language* long before he would have regarded the *Introduction to Semantics* which he later wrote as having a proper subject-matter. For in syntax one studied the internal structure of language, whereas in semantics one undertook the forbidden examination of the relation of language to fact. But this ascetic doctrine was never favoured in England. Instead we find watered-down versions which might be said to illustrate the orthodox British habit of compromise. Thus Wisdom said: 'A fact [i.e., here, a sentence] can only *show* the sense of the fact it expresses. It cannot state it. (I think we might have a sentence which states the sense of a fact which it does not express. Thus "This is characterised by red" seems to state the sense of the fact which not it but "This is red" expresses.)' For Wittgenstein, of course, the concept of characterization is as much a pseudo-concept as is the concept of an object. It denotes nothing.

So much for the notion of picturing on the assumption that we have a perfect language. So far, except for Wittgenstein's stern doctrine of the impossibility of talking about form, there was general agreement among the atomists. But according to Wisdom, picturing is an ideal relation between sentence and fact, almost impossible to attain; most sentences do not picture; picturing is the limit towards which we travel in analysis. For some less perfect forms of expression Wisdom had the name 'sketch', and of the most imperfect utterances of ordinary language he gave no positive doctrine. We need not quarrel with his terminology; but he also says: 'Wittgenstein says that sentences picture facts. But hardly any sentences in ordinary language do picture facts. Wittgenstein does not wish to assert that they do. He is trying

to point out an ideal to which some sentences try to attain.'[1]
Here it seems that Wisdom has just misunderstood Wittgenstein, and about this we must quarrel. Unless our exposition
of him has been quite mistaken, Wittgenstein must have
thought that all sentences pictured, in his sense of picturing;
otherwise one could not understand them. He is continually
saying things like: 'Sentences can be true or false only by
being pictures of reality' (4.06). What Wisdom calls picturing
is what happens when we have, in Wittgenstein's terms, 'a
symbolism which obeys the rules of *logical* grammar—of
logical syntax' (3.525). But in other cases there are still pictures, even if they are misleading ones. What Wittgenstein
said of ordinary language was that the tacit conventions required to understand it were enormously complicated—the
situation is as if we had pictures or maps with queer *ad hoc*
rules of projection; each idiom is liable to employ a rule of
projection different from the next. But this does not mean
that there is in ordinary language no law of projection, and, if
there is one, then there must be similarity of structure. Thus,
though the differences between Wittgenstein and Wisdom
are to a considerable extent only terminological, they are not
only so, and we must be on our guard against misunderstanding Wittgenstein in the way in which Wisdom appears to
have done.

Here we must leave the specific discussion of the doctrine
of picturing. It is a puzzling doctrine. Some of the puzzles
connected with it we have already tried to remove, others we
shall shortly try to deal with by showing the sources of the
doctrine and the way it fits into the general picture of logical
atomism and analysis. But others, more fundamental, can
only be removed by and in the light of a better doctrine of the
relation of language and fact. To provide such a better
account is not within our present scope. Nor would it be an
easy task to undertake.

[1] *Mind*, 1931, p. 202.

6

FURTHER GENERAL COMMENTS ON
LOGICAL ATOMISM

OUR positive exposition of logical atomism is now as complete as the scale of our enterprise warrants. We shall not, however, be leaving it entirely. We shall not proceed to an independent criticism of its doctrines, but we shall be much concerned with the criticisms which were made of it both by other analysts and by the atomists themselves in the light of further reflexion in our next main section. This seems the best method of procedure in trying to exhibit the development of thought about analysis. But before this next main section of this book a short survey of the ground so far covered may be profitable.

Given a general acceptance of an empiricist standpoint, how, it may be asked, do we arrive at logical atomism? One way, in barest outline, is this. As empiricists we will admit, as far as possible, the existence of nothing not vouched for by the senses. But if we examine the subject-matter of the most ordinary discourse we immediately find that we are continually talking about things which we cannot possibly claim to be simple objects of observation, vouched for by sensation in a straightforward manner. We need to speak of states in ordinary political discourse, the social observer speaks of the average family, and so on. It would be much too paradoxical a defence of our position to say that such talk was about nothing, or even that it was about mere figments of the imagination; we therefore take the well-trodden path which Berkeley, Hume, and many others have walked before us. We say that it is, of course, correct to talk about physical objects, but that this is but a shorthand way of speaking about sense-experience; it is correct to speak of states, but only as a shorthand way of speaking about people and their dealings with each other, and so on. Such words as 'Russia' and 'chair' do not really denote objects over and above the objects of sense-experience; all talk not explicitly about sense-experience is either an abbreviation of such talk or it is nonsense. If we wish to prove this contention we are led to practise new-level analysis, by which we try to show how to write out these cryptic statements about sense-experience in unabbreviated form. In the same spirit we practise same-level analysis to dispose of arguments which apparently require us to recognize such entities as the round square and the present King of France.

Thus from one point of view we find that analysis is not a new device of the atomists but rather a traditional procedure of empiricists; the difference is mainly in the extra rigour of theory and increased subtlety of the conceptual apparatus employed. If we ask what the use of such analytic methods involves, it seems that we have to eliminate words or phrases which seem to denote some object but which, through some defect of level or logical form, only appear to, but do not really, do so. Thus we are led to an ideal of having sentences which contain only words which denote some object of sense-experience (of acquaintance, as Russell put it) and regarding all other sentences as either misleading versions of such sentences or else meaningless. We are encouraged in such an enterprise by the success of the mathematical logicians in carrying out a similar programme with regard to mathematics—the most complicated statements of mathematics can apparently be shown to be only short and misleading versions of simple logical statements (misleading here because it appears that mathematicians are talking of objects which are real numbers, or complex numbers, &c.).

But why do we think that such a new way of talking as we are advocating is less misleading, superior to ordinary language? Why do we want to say, for example, that Russell's analysis of descriptions shows the logical form of our statements better than the originals? How can the long set of statements about sense-data be better than the original statement about chairs? Why have we no doubt that if only we can make such translations we have made a genuine philosophical advance? The answer that presented itself as obvious to the logical atomists was that if one form of statement appeared better, less misleading, than another it must be because one represented the facts better than the other. And if one form of statement represents the facts better than another it must do so because it has a structure more similar to the structure of the facts than the other. This is the doctrine of picturing.

That is one way of getting to logical atomism. The metaphysics here appears as the justification of empiricist practice throughout the ages. Our atomic, and only genuine, facts are the facts given in sense-experience; since, as Hume said, we perceive no internal relations between matters of fact, we must depict our facts in an extensional language—Hume's analysis of causation is a model for this—any fact can alter and the rest stay the same. From this point of view we see that logical atomism is not arbitrary but the view of the world which justifies reductive analysis on empiricist lines pursued with complete rigour.

We can get to logical atomism by another route. Now we start from mathematical logic. We start from the very complete logical apparatus which has been devised so triumphantly to act as a basis for all mathematical argument, and notice how few and simple are the types of primitive forms of statement from which we need to start. All but these primitive forms are theoretically superfluous. Now if this logic is sufficient for deriving all forms of argumentation, even the most subtle, and if, as all logical tradition allowed, the statements of logic are the skeletal forms of ordinary statements in abstraction from their content, which is irrelevant to logic, then it seems that all statements which can be used in reasoning, all serious rational statements, must have the form of some statement of logic. Since all these forms can be reduced to a few primitive forms, then all statements must be of forms reducible to these few primitive forms. Thus language must be a collection of statements of the forms of the primitive statements of logic with constants replacing the variables to give content to the statements.

Empiricism now comes in in a subsidiary role as the principle of selection of constants—atomic propositions are those which result from substituting empirical constants for variables in the primitive forms of logic. If all rational statements are included in such a language, then we must suppose that the world can be adequately represented, pictured in such a language. The world deduced in such a way from such a logic as Russell's will be the world of the logical atomists.

We must not ask which of these ways of arriving at logical atomism actually represents the atomists' way of thinking; they are complementary moments in their thinking. But one approach weighed more with some of the atomists than the other. In so far as one starts mainly from the belief that the logic of *Principia Mathematica* contains all the necessary forms of statement, empiricism taking second place, as is true of Russell, then one will be inclined to accept all the primitive elements of that logic as requisite; for example, the quantifier is a primitive idea, and quantified functional logic is not reducible to the calculus of propositions; in other words general propositions are not reducible to sets of singular propositions. Hence Russell does not much mind admitting general facts. But if one starts from the empiricist angle one will wish to eliminate general propositions, since quantifiers denote nothing, and will try to maintain, as Wittgenstein did, that in theory generality is eliminable.

Thus we may see logical atomism as derived, with supplementary hypotheses, from the acceptance of reductive analysis, which atomism justifies, and the belief that in logic one studies the form of the propositions which occur in the arguments of the sciences and ordinary discourse. It is not a figment of the metaphysical imagination working in a void. If one is to talk of logical form, if one is to practise analysis, then one must either be a logical atomist or think up some better justification. We shall soon have to examine some alternatives to atomism which were offered as such justifications, though it will not always be clear that they were improvements.

In a way, logical atomism was not new; there is no gulf of principle between Hume and the philosophers whom we have been considering. But there was an enormous increase in rigour, technical elaboration, and logical resources. Above all, there was the encouraging fact that armed with the new technical resources the traditional reductive practices had secured, it appeared, resounding successes in the field of mathematics. With this model there could be a new hope that with the same scrupulous rigour similar successes would at last be achieved in other fields. This was not the first time in the history of philosophy that philosophical expectations were based on a mathematical foundation; Descartes, for example, had done the same. In the past such foundations had turned out to be little better than sand.

PART II

LOGICAL POSITIVISM AND THE DOWNFALL OF LOGICAL ATOMISM

THE life of this classical logical atomism was short, in spite of the brilliant philosophical gifts of Russell, Wittgenstein, Wisdom, and its other adherents. There was, for example, no further writing which could conceivably be called ortho-dox after Wisdom's papers on logical constructions. Nor was it simply that new men with new ideas came to the centre of the stage, for logical atomism was abandoned by its most faithful followers. We must now, therefore, turn to consider the question why logical atomism so suddenly lost its place in English philosophy. To this question there are, I think, two principal answers.

First of all, many of its actual and potential adherents came to suspect, for reasons which we shall soon examine, that metaphysics as a whole and as such must be rejected; from this point of view logical atomism had to go, not because it was defective as metaphysics, but because it was metaphysics at all. This view was so quickly and so generally persuasive partly because the arguments for it had been already worked out in some detail in Vienna.

The other principal explanation of the fall of atomism was the discovery, one by one, of specific defects in the meta-physics, gradually leading to the conclusion that it must be abandoned as failing to do the job it was trying to do.

We shall have to elaborate each of these two answers in turn, but before we examine either of them in detail there are some general points which must be noticed. First, we must observe that both these lines of criticism were developed within the

movement itself. Logical atomism fell to self-criticism, not
to an attack from outside. In general, there was no outside
attack which was sufficiently informed and sympathetic to
have any effect. Merely hostile criticism rarely has any effect
in philosophy, and for very good reasons. Admittedly the
main attack on metaphysics as such came from philosophers
whom we have not previously discussed, the Vienna Circle
and their associates. But the Vienna Circle had always been
regarded as allies by British analysts, and also the views of the
Circle on this matter were based largely on Wittgenstein's
Tractatus, by which they had been profoundly influenced.

Another point is this. It might with considerable justification be thought that the two lines of criticism of logical
atomism, that it was to be discarded outright merely as
metaphysics and that it contained specific defects, however
serious, were mutually exclusive. If a philosopher is going
to condemn atomism outright as a special case of metaphysics,
it might well be thought that he will have no truck with any
detailed criticism of its special metaphysical doctrines; for a
willingness to indulge in detailed criticism apparently implies
a belief that there is a criterion of good and bad metaphysics, certainly that metaphysics is intelligible. One cannot
make detailed corrections in what is radically mistaken and
even nonsensical. To put the other aspect of the matter, one
would not expect that those who made objections to the
details of a metaphysical doctrine would be willing to agree
that a general attack on metaphysics was legitimate. The two
positions are indeed incompatible, and it would be inconsistent to attempt to combine the two criticisms into a single
whole; to do so would be like Berkeley's rejection of the idea
of material substance as nonsensical in combination with a rejection of it as superfluous and a slight on the omnipotence of
God. Clearly one cannot have it both ways. It would, however,
be a definite mistake to think that individual philosophers
in forming their views cannot be influenced by incompatible

considerations. Berkeley would not, I suspect, have regarded the idea of material substance as a 'manifest repugnancy' if he had not also found it to be superfluous; and if that sounds odd it is only partly because philosophers are not entirely consistent, and very largely because to find a notion both nonsensical and superfluous is not quite as inconsistent as it appears to be if it is a philosopher who is calling a well-established philosophical term nonsensical. Nonsense is itself a very metaphysical concept. In the same way as in the case of Berkeley the detailed objections to atomism and the general rejection of metaphysics worked on philosophers simultaneously; they would not have been so willing to regard metaphysics as meaningless if they had not begun to find flaws in logical atomism, and they would probably have made much more strenuous efforts to meet the detailed criticisms and repair the flaws if they had not begun to suspect the whole metaphysical enterprise. Thus the two sorts of attack, though logically distinct and even incompatible, are not to be considered in complete isolation and identified exclusively with particular groups of philosophers.

One further preliminary remark, this time about our own method. There were a large number of presuppositions which were common property to the atomists and their immediate critics. The atomists *were* their own immediate critics, and they did not become completely new men in a day. We shall not at this stage deal critically with, or even attempt to bring into the open, those common presuppositions. We shall confine ourselves to those criticisms of atomism which were made at the time, though not necessarily aiming at an exact fidelity of emphasis and vocabulary. We shall start by considering the arguments for the general rejection of metaphysics and the alternative view of the nature of analysis proposed by those who rejected the metaphysical justification provided by logical atomism.

7

THE REJECTION OF METAPHYSICS

THE rejection of metaphysics as such is not a new phenomenon which occurred for the first time in the present century.
Even in the ancient world the sceptics and the empiricists had
considered the gaining of metaphysical knowledge to be
impossible; in a high-flown, but not untypical, passage
Hume had consigned all metaphysics to the flames as worthless; Kant had likened the attempt to construct a metaphysical system to the beating of wings in the void; Comte
had rejected metaphysics as a stage on the road to positive
science which the world had now outgrown. But though the
rejection of metaphysics is not a new thing, the grounds
offered for its rejection which we have now to consider are
substantially novel. Most, at least, of the earlier objectors
had maintained that metaphysics must be abandoned because
we had no means of deciding what answer to its perfectly
significant questions was correct or because it set about
answering them in a mistaken, unscientific manner; metaphysics was practically impossible or worthless because we
could not test the truth or falsity of its statements, but its
statements were at least intelligible. But now the objection
was made that metaphysical questions and answers are one
and all nonsensical; metaphysics is not worthless, idle speculation, but pseudo-speculation. Hume had indeed anticipated
this position, but only in *obiter dicta*, and as a rhetorical
flourish, not as a fully worked-out thesis. The emphatic,
clear-cut distinction between idle speculation and nonsense
disguised as speculation was not made before the twentieth
century. Speculation which is idle, because untestable in
practice, as would be the speculation what Socrates ate
on his fifth birthday, is now sharply distinguished from

pseudo-speculation; in the latter case we are not merely unable to determine the truth or falsity of a thesis, for there is no genuine thesis to be true or false.

Thus the grounds for rejecting metaphysics we are now to consider are in a way new, since they are the first working out of a thesis; but since the roots go deep they are in a way old. Previous philosophers had time and time again said things which had the rejection of all metaphysics as unintelligible as an inevitable consequence, even though the consequence was not drawn. This is a common phenomenon in philosophy. If, as some of the British philosophers of the seventeenth and eighteenth centuries had maintained, all the objects of the human understanding are ideas of sensation, memory, and imagination, or passions accessible to reflexion, then understanding ceases if we try to talk about anything else. But this conclusion was not drawn in a systematic way. None the less, a doctrine which draws the conclusion from a viewpoint with which one is well acquainted is easier to assimilate than one whose roots are less deep in the past.

Wittgenstein is the basic source for the anti-metaphysical attack on atomism, as he is for atomism itself. It is not merely that he later criticized the doctrine of the *Tractatus*, though no doubt he did; certainly the criticisms contained in *Philosophical Investigations* are irrelevant to the present stage of our inquiry. The criticisms with which we are now concerned are to be found in the *Tractatus* itself, alongside the atomistic doctrines. Having said in his preface: 'The truth of the thoughts communicated here seems to me unassailable and definitive. I am, therefore, of the opinion that the problems have in essentials been finally solved', he goes on to say in his concluding remarks: 'My propositions are elucidatory in this way: he who understands me finally recognises them as senseless, when he has used them to climb out beyond them. (He must so to speak throw away the ladder, after he has climbed up on it.) He must surmount these propositions;

then he sees the world rightly. Whereof one cannot speak, thereof must one be silent.'

It will be useful to collect together at this stage some of the earlier remarks of Wittgenstein which lead up to and prepare the reader for this conclusion.

4.003   Most propositions and questions, that have been written about philosophical matters, are not false, but nonsensical. We cannot therefore answer questions of this kind at all, but only state their senselessness. Most questions and propositions of the philosophers result from the fact that we do not understand the logic of our language. . . . And so it is not to be wondered at that the deepest problems are really no problems.

4.0031   All philosophy is 'Critique of language'.

4.1   A proposition exhibits the existence and non-existence of atomic facts.

4.11   The totality of true propositions is the total natural science. . . .

4.111   Philosophy is not one of the natural sciences. (The word 'philosophy' must mean something which stands above or below, but not beside the natural sciences.)

4.112   The object of philosophy is the logical clarification of thoughts. Philosophy is not a doctrine but an activity. A philosophical work consists entirely of elucidations. The result of philosophy is not a number of philosophical propositions, but to make propositions clear. Philosophy should make clear and delimit sharply the thoughts which otherwise are, as it were, opaque and blurred.

6.4   All propositions are of equal value.

6.42   Hence also there can be no ethical propositions. Propositions cannot express anything higher.

6.421   It is clear that ethics cannot be expressed. Ethics is transcendental.

6.53   The right method of philosophy would be this. To say nothing except what can be said, i.e. the propositions of natural science, i.e. something that has nothing to do with philosophy; and then always, when someone else wished to say something metaphysical, to demonstrate to him that he has given no meaning to certain signs in his propositions. This method would be unsatisfying to the other—he would not have the feeling that we were teaching him philosophy— but it would be the only strictly correct method.

There we have the summary of the anti-metaphysical strain in the *Tractatus*. The only significant propositions are the propositions of the natural sciences (interpreted widely to include all possible data of science, e.g. such statements as 'This is red'). In particular we cannot say how these propositions are related to the world (for what is shown cannot be said), or what makes a proposition true or false, and so on. There are no philosophical propositions. In the course of the book Wittgenstein has indeed been saying all these unsayable things, but consciously regarding them as nonsense. By saying them he hopes to make clear why one cannot say them. Here there is clearly a full-size paradox. The definitive solution of a question must not be nonsense, and Wittgenstein had been claiming to provide a definitive solution.

This quotation from Ramsey represents a pretty obvious reaction to the paradoxical tension in Wittgenstein's position:

Philosophy must be of some use and we must take it seriously. It must clear our thoughts and so our actions. Or else it is a disposition we have to check, and an enquiry to see that this is so; i.e. the chief proposition of philosophy is that philosophy is nonsense. And again we must then take seriously that it is nonsense, and not pretend, as Wittgenstein does, that it is important nonsense!

Now for a long time, as we have already seen, the general reaction in England was to take the line that metaphysics was legitimate, provided that it was critical and not speculative. Wittgenstein's own metaphysics was regarded as critical; it was therefore regarded as in principle, at least, acceptable, and his characterization of it as nonsense was rejected. In particular it was not accepted that talk of the relation of language to the world was impossible. We have been looking at things from such a point of view for the greater part of the time. But others resolved the paradox in the opposite direction. Wittgenstein's rejection of metaphysics was accepted and metaphysics was therefore, at least in intention, thrown overboard. This line was taken very early on in Vienna, where the old positivist tradition was strong; it was not until about the time of Ayer's *Language Truth and Logic*, and largely then through the agency of that book, that it gained any wide currency in England.

A short digression into pure history might be useful at this stage. Wittgenstein began his serious philosophical career as a philosopher in Cambridge before the First World War, where he was a pupil of Russell's, though he quickly came to influence Russell as much as Russell influenced him. He returned to Austria before the war, in which he took part, but during which the *Tractatus* none the less got written. The *Tractatus* was there first published in German. There were at that time a number of empirically-minded philosophers, with a close interest in science, centred on Vienna, notably Schlick, Carnap, Hahn, Waismann, and Neurath. They had been much influenced by the positivist (old type) Mach and also by the logical and mathematical writings of Russell. They seized on the *Tractatus* and worked on it hard, having also a certain amount of personal contact with Wittgenstein though he never joined in their general discussions. This group formally constituted themselves as the Vienna Circle in 1922, giving the name of Logical Positivism, or Logical Empiricism, to their viewpoint. Already disposed to reject metaphysics on the old positivist grounds that it was an immature precursor of science, they readily accepted the anti-metaphysical strain in Wittgenstein, calling themselves logical positivists or logical empiricists to emphasize their acceptance of the view of Wittgenstein that metaphysics was not merely outdated as the old positivism had it, but was a logically impossible enterprise, being excluded by the essential nature of language; it was positivism on logical grounds. When Wittgenstein returned to Cambridge in the middle twenties, this movement went on in Austria in comparative isolation from the English work for a number of years. In the very late twenties their influence began to be felt in England. In the early thirties Ayer visited Vienna and joined in their discussions. Largely through him, and Miss Stebbing, their work became well known here in the early thirties. So much for pure and simple history.

What, then, are the grounds for the rejection of metaphysics? Such a rejection is already implicit in the basic doctrines of atomism, as we have seen. If all statements are truth-functions of elementary propositions which report observations then they will all be either empirical themselves or else tautologies or contradictions. But metaphysical statements do not seem to be classifiable under any of these heads. But if we are to gain a fuller understanding of the grounds for the rejection of metaphysics we must turn to consider the notorious verification principle. The verification principle is not essentially a very novel or obscure doctrine except in its traditional formulation. This formulation is that the meaning of a statement is the method of its verification. Consequently to know the meaning of a statement, to understand it, is to know how to verify it; and an additional consequence is that if there is no way of verifying a proposition at all it has no meaning. Therefore metaphysical propositions, and quite a number of other linguistic performances which have usually been counted as meaningful, turn out to be nonsensical.

Hume is an ancestor of this, as of most other, empiricist doctrines; it will help us to understand it if we start from him. As an oversimplification we can say that Hume held that the only possible objects of the human mind are impressions.

Hence for a word to have a meaning it must be one which refers to an impression (in his own language 'all ideas must be copies of impressions'). Hence any intelligible sentence must refer only to possible impressions; for how is one to understand a word which has not been learnt ultimately by means of ostensive definition? Thus to know the meaning of a word is to know with what type of impression it is linked by ostensive definition. This seems to be the kernel of Hume's doctrine on this point after the psychological husk has been stripped from it. Now if we call Hume's doctrine that the objects of human experience, the ultimate particulars, are impressions his metaphysical thesis, we see that the metaphysics of logical atomism in Wittgenstein's version differed from it mainly in the substitution of sensibly given facts for sensibly given particulars as the ultimate data. We can now see the verification principle as involving a corresponding reformulation of Hume's epistemological thesis that all meaningful words must be ostensively definable. We may put it schematically thus:—

Old empiricism (Hume)
  Metaphysical thesis: All objects are sense-given.
New empiricism (logical positivism)
  Metaphysical thesis: All facts are sense-given.
Old empiricism
  Epistemological thesis: All significant words are names of sense-given objects.
New empiricism
  Epistemological thesis: All significant sentences describe sensible fact.

Now the old empiricism, with all its difficulties, was plausible enough to gain many adherents; but the new version is much more plausible. For the minimum self-contained unit of speech is the sentence (which may, of course, be a sentence containing but one word); Hume could not explain plausibly how such words as 'all', 'and', 'if', and 'but' have a meaning, but now we can say that a word has a meaning if it does a job in a sentence, whatever job that may be. The verification principle, it appears, can explain what it is for a sentence or a word to have a meaning.

The verification principle can be stated as a consequence of the atomic hypothesis in metaphysics; Wittgenstein hinted at this without an explicit statement in the *Tractatus*. If the only genuine facts are atomic facts then every significant sentence must be analysable into pictures of atomic facts. Hence to understand a sentence is to know what atomic facts must obtain for it to be true; and to know this is to know how to verify it. But it is clearly undesirable to derive an anti-metaphysical principle from a metaphysical doctrine in this paradoxical way. Moreover, since the metaphysics is the picture of the world which seems to be implied by an empiricist epistemology in combination with Russellian logic, it is undesirable to present a major epistemological thesis as a consequence of metaphysics. So we must be able to give a direct epistemological justification of the verification principle: and to give a plausible one is not hard.

Let us suppose that we are put into a milieu where a technical vocabulary is used which we do not understand, and let us suppose that nobody explains to us the meaning of the technical statements in terms of the language that we do know; could we come to understand what these people say? Clearly we could, answers the positivist, in principle always, in practice in simpler cases, provided that the technical language is empirical. We may perhaps have had no previous experience of rugby football and start going to watch games, where we overhear people's comments, but have no expert interpreter with us. At first we shall hear such remarks as 'He was off-side' or 'He missed his tackle' without understanding them at all. But if we go on watching, listening when these things are said, and noting when they are accepted or rejected by other experts, i.e. observing what counts as a verification of them and what a falsification, we shall get at first a rough, and later an exact, understanding of them. When, and only when, I have learnt what empirical circumstance verifies and what falsifies the statement 'He has missed his tackle', then I understand the statement. There is nothing else required. We could, of course, have learnt quicker by a verbal explanation; but what would the verbal explanation be? Something like this: 'He flung himself at, or tried to catch hold of, the man with the ball, and has failed to touch him, or has failed to hold on to him'—and this is to give the method of verification in words, in a complex of statements whose meaning I must in any case have learnt by the direct method of observing what situations verify them. Now it is clear that in some very complicated matters no one person in a single lifetime could come to understand without the aid of verbal explanations; perhaps this is true of modern science; but this makes no difference in theory—one is merely using a short cut. It is clear that we must start by learning to understand some sentences by directly observing their method of verification before the short cut of verbal explanation can be used at all. Surely that is how as babies we make our first steps to an understanding of language? That is how we so quickly learn, in spite of all efforts by our parents to prevent us, the meaning of 'There is chocolate in the sweet-tin'.

But let us now suppose that the technical statements that we are brought up against are the technical statements of metaphysicians; one perhaps claims that tables are substances and the other denies it, or one advocates psychophysical parallelism, the other interactionism. How are we to learn the meaning of these statements? There is no method of verification to be learnt, since the empirical expectations of the disputing metaphysicians are the same. All we can have is a closed circle of verbal explanations and perhaps a delusive feeling of comprehension because the question whether two processes are merely simultaneous or interacting can be an empirical one with a method of verification, as when we investigate whether something was or was not a coincidence. If we think that we understand the metaphysicians we deceive ourselves. One of the jobs of the philosopher is to show how language can so deceive intelligent people.

Such in outline is the meaning and defence of the verification principle. Even such an abbreviated defence and exposition ought to be sufficient to show how it might easily be accepted. Its apparent simplicity was not its least attraction; it was also a relief to the harder-headed philosopher to be told that the apparently insuperable difficulties of deep metaphysics were a tissue of pseudo-problems requiring no answer.

But this apparently simple theory had different detailed forms, notably those called the weak and the strong verification principles. Each of these had its attractions and its drawbacks. If we accept the epistemological correlate of the extreme atomistic hypothesis held by Wittgenstein according to which the only facts are particular atomic facts, and there are no general facts, for example, then we shall hold the strong verification principle. According to this version of the principle any statement, to be significant, must be, in principle, capable of being conclusively verified or falsified; every proposition is a truth-function of a set of simple statements all of which could in principle be checked and the truth or falsehood of the proposition thus conclusively established. It is not good enough that some evidence should appear to be relevant. In defence of this version it could be urged that it alone was compatible with a thorough-going truth-functional view of language. Or, epistemologically, we can say that as to know the meaning of a statement is to know the method of its verification, then to the extent that it cannot be verified it cannot be understood. How, if a statement is only partly verifiable, are we to understand it in so far as it is not verifiable? There would thus appear to be strong reasons for holding that if one holds the verification principle at all one must hold it in the strong version.

But there were also difficulties, and formidable ones, for the strong version of the verification principle. We have already considered the great difficulties presented to logical atomism by general propositions, which it seemed impossible to regard as truth-functions of atomic propositions, so that Russell, at one extreme, considered himself obliged to recognize the existence of general facts, and Ramsey, at the other, to deny that so-called general propositions are propositions at all. We have now come to the parallel difficulty for the verification principle: how could a general proposition be conclusively verifiable? In general the same heroic course that Ramsey took on logical grounds was taken by upholders of the strong verification principle on epistemological grounds. 'If not truth-functions of elementary propositions, then not propositions', said Ramsey; 'If not conclusively verifiable in principle, then not propositions', said Schlick. Here is a translation of some of his own words:

Natural laws do not have the character of propositions which are true or false but rather set forth instructions for the formation of such propositions. . . . Natural laws are not general implications because they cannot be verified for all cases; they are rather directions, rules of behaviour, for the investigator to find his way about in reality, to anticipate certain events. . . . We should not forget that observations and experiments are acts by means of which we enter into direct connection with nature. The relations between reality and ourselves frequently stand in sentences which have the grammatical form of assertions but whose essential sense consists in the fact that they are directions for possible acts.[1]

This is very like the doctrine in Ramsey's paper, 'Variable Hypotheticals', already discussed, though Ramsey's grounds were logical, Schlick's a theory of meaning. Both cut their

---

[1] *Der Kausalität in der gegenwartigen Physik*; translated by Weinberg, *Examination of Logical Positivism*, p. 146.

way out of a difficulty by treating general propositions as rules rather than as statements. But before we hastily dismiss Schlick's views about natural laws as unrealistic tampering with science by a philosopher, we should recall that he came to philosophy as a trained physicist.

An interesting alternative was suggested by Karl Popper in his book *Die Logik der Forschung*, one largely designed to deal with the difficulty of verifying universal propositions. Popper suggested that the criterion of significance should be taken to be falsifiability instead of verifiability. Since a singular proposition 'This A is not B', if true, conclusively falsifies the general proposition 'All As are B', this disposes of the difficulty about regarding statements of natural law as meaningful. But there is a compensating difficulty in Popper's view. For just as universal propositions are conclusively falsifiable but not conclusively verifiable, so existential propositions are conclusively verifiable but not falsifiable; if we can find but one (or, perhaps, two) As that are B we have conclusively verified that *some As are B*, whereas it is clear that however many As we find that are not B we have not conclusively falsified that some are. We can in fact easily construct a statement which is neither conclusively falsifiable nor conclusively verifiable by making it contain both the unverifiable 'all' and the unfalsifiable 'some'; an example would be the statement that every person who walks under a ladder will meet with some misfortune.

According to the weak form of the verification principle a proposition is significant if there are some observations which would be relevant to its truth or falsity. This allows for the significance of general propositions, since it is clear that we can at least find evidence for and against them. It was also considered by its advocates to have another advantage, namely, that if we come to hold that no proposition is logically incorrigible we must adopt a weak form of the verification principle for all propositions, quite apart from the difficulty about general propositions, since no propositions whatsoever will be conclusively verifiable. It seemed, moreover, that there were considerable grounds for holding this view since the possibility of hallucination, illusion, misdescription, and even slips of the tongue might lead us into error about the simplest matter of fact; in practice, too, the scientist sometimes rejects an observation as erroneous rather than abandoning the theory with which the statement of observation conflicts.

Supporters of this form of the verification principle ran into very serious difficulties in their attempts to give a precise formulation of it; clearly it was insufficient to speak merely of observations relevant to truth or falsity, as metaphysicians were quick to point out by claiming that they thought that observations were in some way relevant to their metaphysical theories. Most formulations were quickly shown to exclude as meaningless much that the positivists did not wish to exclude, or to include as meaningful the most blatant nonsense. It was also hard to find a formulation which did not seem to include too much in the meaning of a statement; it was difficult, for example, to exclude what one will find written in recent history books from the meaning of the statement that Queen Anne is dead. Further, if one regarded observations of what happened in the eighteenth century as in principle impossible for us today it seemed hard to include in the meaning of such a statement what seemed most vital to it. A candid discussion of many of these difficulties will be found in the Introduction to the second edition of Ayer's *Language Truth and Logic*. Since other more fundamental difficulties to be discussed later are more important for our purposes we shall not discuss further these difficulties of comparative difficulty, which it always seemed possible might be overcome by better formulation of the principle.

8

LOGICAL POSITIVISM AND ANALYSIS

THE metaphysics of logical atomism and the conception of analysis which went with it had been, as we have seen, complementary. Roughly, the metaphysics had been the justification of the method of analysis, and the metaphysics had in turn determined the exact nature of the ideal to which analysis had to conform. It is important to realize that the logical positivists, while they rejected the metaphysics, took over the conception of analysis more or less complete. The actual practice of analysis went on always while the justification and characterization of it changed. Moore, after all, was neither a positivist nor an atomist, yet he practised the same sort of analysis as they did and was even regarded as the leading exponent of the technique. It was always obscurely felt that analysis, which overtly consisted in replacing one form of words by another with the same meaning, was a proper philosophical pursuit, and that there was good reason for preferring one form of words to another; it was only when it came to saying why analysis was a proper pursuit, why one form of words was preferable to another, that really serious differences arose. The atomists had given the justification that the new form of words better pictured the structure of reality; but that answer certainly could not be given by a positivist, though we may suspect that in fact this metaphysical view still had some power over him.

We must now, therefore, examine the accounts given by the positivists of the nature of analysis; we must see how they tried to show that analysis was a legitimate and, moreover, valuable activity without making any metaphysical presuppositions and without making any metaphysical statements. On a great deal there was virtual unanimity amongst the positivists, and it will be convenient to deal with that portion of their doctrine first. Then we must come to some questions which were of special difficulty for them, and at this point we shall notice some divergence of opinion.

We already know that the logical positivists, like Hume, claimed that all legitimate uses of language were either synthetic and *a posteriori*, i.e. empirical, or were tautologies. The empirical propositions were those of the natural sciences, understood to include the factual statements of everyday life; the tautologies are typically what we meet in the exact sciences such as mathematics. Wittgenstein had said, and the logical positivists agreed, that there were no special propositions of philosophy, metaphysical or otherwise. Philosophy was not a science alongside the natural sciences. Clearly therefore the philosopher does not make empirical statements. But analysis does not consist of empirical statements. The form of an analysis is the assertion of an equivalence between two expressions; we may say that 'The present King of France is bald' is equivalent to 'There is one and only one thing which, &c.', or that 'The average plumber earns £10 per week' is equivalent to 'The number of pounds earned each week by plumbers divided by the number of plumbers, &c.'. But a statement of an equivalence is, if correct, a tautology, if incorrect, a contradiction. So if a philosopher sticks to making analyses he will avoid either infringing on the preserves of natural science or attempting to make a special sort of philosophical statement. Philosophy is therefore to be identified with analysis. Analysis is the one and only legitimate activity of philosophers.

But the question now arises why analysis should be done. The logical atomist would have agreed that his analyses, if correct, had the verbal form of equivalences, but he said that the point of it was analysis of fact, the clarification of the structure and inter-relationships of facts, and thus of the world. But the logical positivists could not say this. Instead they simply denied any ulterior motive and claimed that philosophy was the analysis and clarification of language as such; or, since the purpose of a language is that we may make scientific statements, the clarification of the language of science.

Still conceiving a language to be a calculus with an added vocabulary—constants—to replace the variables of the calculus, the positivists envisaged their task in analysis as the exhibition in strings of tautologies of the structure of a language. There would be a set of sentences of simple form and containing only the basic vocabulary (such as the atomists had thought to picture basic facts) and out of them would be constructed the whole language of science; or to put the matter in reverse order, analysis would reduce the whole language of science to the basic elements out of which it was built. In the course of this analysis the relation between statements of observation, laws, hypotheses, and theories would be exhibited as would that of the more rarified, higher-order, concepts to the simpler ones. Most of the time of course the analyst would, in a less grandiose way, be attempting to straighten up the analysis of one portion of language at a comparatively high level; but Carnap, in his *Logische Aufbau der Welt*, went so far as to attempt to give a sketch of how the language of science could be analysed in terms of sentences containing only names of primitive experiences and the single relation *memory of similarity* (*Ähnlichkeitserrinerung*). If challenged for a reason for this activity the positivist claimed that apart from the intrinsic interest of his results two advantages were secured. First, an analysis of the language of science was likely to be of use to the scientist, especially in the frontier regions of progress—perhaps an earlier analysis would, for example, have revealed the ambiguity in the concept of simultaneity which it was left to Einstein to discover; this was a logical, not a physical discovery. Secondly, if we do not understand language thoroughly we are always liable to misuse it; in particular, we are liable to fall into metaphysics. Thus analysis will be a prophylactic against linguistic abuses. It can be no small thing to understand the tool of all sciences and all skills, and understanding of a language is achieved by analysis.

We have now added two principal theses of logical positivism to the rejection of metaphysics and the verification principle. First, philosophy is to be identified with analysis. This, of course, is not intended to deny that any but the most rigorous works will contain empirical statements about what other philosophers have said, about what the writer is going to discuss next, and so on. But these will be, strictly speaking, historical, not philosophical, sentences. Secondly, philosophy is nothing more and nothing less than the analysis of language; and since analysis is done in sets of equivalences, which are tautologies, philosophy is even to be equated with logic.

Thus the old activity of analysis can go on undisturbed. We can even continue to speak of logical constructions, since to say that Xs are logical constructions out of Ys is but a way of saying that 'X' is an incomplete symbol replaceable (though not simply replaceable) by 'Y', i.e. it is in fact part of linguistic analysis and not really about Xs and Ys at all. Though the positivist would now reject the atomists' account of the nature of analysis, Ayer, in his Preface to *Language Truth and Logic*, was able to recognize even Moore's analysis as being the same task as he set himself. Thus the positivist who did not wish to break too finally with tradition could maintain that Hume in his analysis of causation, Berkeley in his analysis of physical objects, even Plato in, say, his analysis of knowledge in the *Theaetetus*, were doing philosophy as the positivists conceived it, even if they made mistakes of comparative detail in so doing and gave a wrong account of what they were doing. The business is still the old reductive analysis, even if it is under new management.

It might be thought that such a characterization of positivistic analysis embodied an illegitimate nostalgia, and was at least exaggerated. Not merely is a new rationale of analysis being given, but the new talk, when doing analysis, is of words, sentences, and the like—is talk about language, whereas the old analysis used metaphysical pseudo-concepts such as 'thing', 'fact', and the like. It was nonsensical, surely, according to the new régime, and that indicates a big difference. But as a matter of fact most positivists agreed that this difference was largely illusory, as can be shown by means of a new technical term evolved by Carnap in his *Logical Syntax of Language*. It is possible, said Carnap, to talk of language explicitly, by means of quotation marks. If one does so, then we have the formal mode of speech. But there is in ordinary language a device to enable us to talk about language without explicit mention of expressions and without the occurrence of quotation marks. This is the material mode of speech; and what it is can best be made clear by means of examples. Here is a collection of statements, all of which would be said by Carnap to be about language; those in the right-hand column will be so explicitly, and so in the formal mode of speech; those in the left-hand column will be in the material mode, and thus apparently about things other than words.

Material mode	*Formal mode*
A rose is a thing.	'Rose' is a thing-word (substantive, noun).
It is a fact that the rose is red.	'The rose is red' is a sentence (statement).
Redness is a quality.	'Red' is an adjective.
Five is a number.	'Five' is a numeral.

As we shall soon see, Carnap wished to use this distinction for purposes which did not satisfy all positivists; but most agreed in principle to it.

Thus the material mode of speech is a way of speaking which looks like talk about things but is in fact talk about words. If we accept this doctrine we can say that even formerly philosophers who apparently talked about facts, objects, and the like were really talking about language, doing logical syntax, not talking metaphysics, even if they were sometimes not clear, or even positively mistaken, about what they were doing. It is only dangerous, not wrong, to use the material mode of speech. We are permitted, even by Carnap, to continue to use the material mode of speech, provided we do it very carefully and remember that we are doing so. He used it himself, not always too successfully. There are lots of statements in Carnap which certainly are neither empirical nor in the formal mode, and which we should presume are in the material mode; but they are very hard to translate, sometimes, into the formal mode.

Incidentally, Carnap thought that the existence of the material mode of speech was a potent source of metaphysics; philosophers, he considered, used the pseudo-concepts of the material mode (thing, quality, fact, &c.) as though they were genuine concepts. This metaphysical, nonsensical character could be brought out by attempting the translation into the formal mode which ought to be possible. He gave examples in *Logical Syntax of Language*. Thus Wittgenstein's famous mystical 'There is also the inexpressible' was translated into 'There are also words which are not words'. 'Some matters are beyond comprehension' would presumably become 'Some statements are not statements'. Of course a mere 'This matter is to me incomprehensible' goes intelligibly into the formal mode as 'I cannot understand this sentence'. This misuse of the material mode of speech was not, however, regarded as being by any means the only source of metaphysical error. There were other kinds of bad syntax into which we could fall.

That is the agreed part of the new rationale of analysis. Instead of clarifying the logical structure of the world by showing how all facts are complicated clusters of atomic, elementary, or basic facts, and exhibiting the logical structure of these facts and clusters, we now have a clarification of the structure of the language of science. And this clarification is achieved by showing how that language is built up out of the basic or protocol sentences, the logical derivation from which of all other kinds of sentence, including those containing the most complex concepts, must be exhibited and their epistemological relationships made clear. Language is still conceived of as truth-functional in character, and the most abstract of physical theories must therefore be shown to be reducible to basic, protocol statements, and to be validated by them.

But if we are clear what is to be done once we have our protocol statements, the question still remains how we are to identify the underived protocols among the mass of statements and which protocols are to be accepted and which are to be rejected. Now though there was disagreement among the positivists on the exact specifications of a basic protocol, just as there had been disagreement among the atomists on the exact specification of the basic propositions which pictured atomic facts, none the less they clearly wished to select as protocols those statements which had been selected as pictures of atomic facts by the atomists. The question was why these rather than others should be selected. Now Schlick, Ayer, and many other positivists answered substantially that sentences of this sort were to be accepted as protocols because direct reports of experience were of this type and that among protocols those which correctly recorded experience were to be accepted, the rest rejected. 'This is red' is the right sort of sentence to be a protocol because I might have an experience which could be recorded in those words, 'England is hypocritical' is not because it reports no direct experience; I choose between the possible protocols 'This is red' and 'This is green' by seeing which correctly reports experience. Protocols are direct reports of the given and are justified with reference to the given. Whether these reports could be inaccurate, whether they were corrigible, was disputed even in this group, but their direct justification by experience was agreed. Without such a basis, it was maintained, the claim of logical positivism, alternatively styled logical empiricism, to be an empiricist position must be abandoned.

But this position was not acceptable to all positivists; notably Carnap and Neurath rejected it at the period we are now considering. Though the views of Carnap and Neurath are hardly part of the history of British philosophy, and few British philosophers, if any, followed them, this period of their views was such an instructive warning against an over-syntactical approach to philosophy, to British as to other philosophers, that we must consider what they had to say on this topic.

Let us consider the statement: 'Protocol statements are direct records of the given.' Is it a tautology? Surely not, if it is to serve the purpose for which it was intended. No doubt a protocol might be thus defined; but if one means by a protocol sentence a sentence from which other scientific sentences are logically derived but which is not itself derived from any other sentences, which is roughly the explanation usually given, and then, when asked how science gains its protocol sentences, answers that science accepts as protocols those sentences which are records of direct experience, this cannot be a tautology if it is to count as an answer at all. Is it then a statement of empirical science? But while a psychologist might talk of the causal relationship between the uttering of certain sentences and experience, this is a statement of a different kind; and philosophers have no business to be making empirical statements. It seems, then, that taken at face value it is metaphysics—nonsense. Moreover, it is that kind of metaphysics against which Wittgenstein gave an explicit warning (which he himself ignored), it is the attempt to talk about the relation of language to fact. *This* is not clarification of language. Faced with this difficulty most logical empiricists went on saying what they had said, hoping to find a way out of the dilemma. But there were no such half-way houses which suited Carnap and Neurath. They were determined to confine philosophy to logical syntax. Their extraordinarily unplausible attempts to do so must now be followed through. Lest parody be suspected we shall let them speak in their own words so far as possible. The critical comments also will be largely based on Ayer's contemporary paper, 'Verification and Experience'.[1]

In order [said Carnap[2]] to characterise a definite *language* it is necessary to give its *vocabulary* and *syntax*, i.e. the words which occur in it and the rules in accordance with which (1) sentences can be formed from those words and (2) such sentences can be transformed into other sentences, either of the same or of another language (the so-called rules of inference and rules for translation). But is it not also necessary, in order to understand the 'sense' of the sentences, to indicate the 'meaning' of the words? No; the demand thereby made in the material mode is satisfied by giving the formal rules which constitute its syntax. For the 'meaning' of a word is given either by translation or by definition. A translation is a rule for transforming a word from one language to another (e.g. 'cheval' = 'horse'); a definition is a rule for mutual transformation of words in the same language. This is true both of so-called nominal definitions (e.g. 'elephant' = 'animal with such and such distinguishing characteristics') and also, a fact usually forgotten, for so-called ostensive definitions (e.g. 'elephant' = 'animal of the same kind as the animal in this or that position in space-time'); both definitions are translations of words.

We may pause here to observe that Carnap, in his anxiety not to allow that ostensive definition involves the pernicious comparison of language with fact, here perpetrates a first-class howler. Let us suppose that someone points to an elephant at Whipsnade and says 'That is an elephant', in order to let his hearer know the meaning of the word 'elephant'. Let us grant to Carnap that this is much the same as to say 'The animal just on the right of the entrance to Whipsnade now (or "on the 1st of January, 1954") is an elephant', which it certainly is not. Even so the speaker is certainly not saying that the word 'elephant' means the same as 'animal of the same kind as the animal on the right of the entrance to Whipsnade on the 1st of January, 1954'. Yet Carnap says that a definition is a rule for mutual transformation of words in the same language. But in any case the pointing and uttering of the word 'elephant' is not the equivalent of Carnap's sentence. One can teach a foreigner the meaning of the word 'elephant' by pointing to one and saying 'elephant', but not by verbally giving in English the spatio-temporal co-ordinates of an elephant with one's hands in one's pockets.

Having thus tried to establish that the meaning of words is something which one can study without going beyond the bounds of language, Carnap goes on[1] to say some of the forbidden things, but not inadvertently, for he has an explanation in waiting:

Science is a system based on direct experience, and controlled by experimental verification. Verification is based on 'protocol statements', a term whose meaning will be made clearer in the course of further discussion. The term is understood to include statements belonging to the basic protocol or direct record of a scientist's experience. . . . A 'primitive' protocol will be understood to exclude all statements obtained indirectly by induction or otherwise and postulates therefore a sharp (theoretical) distinction between the raw material of scientific investigation and its organisation. . . . .

This may sound sufficiently compromising, but he apparently commits himself even more deeply by adding: 'The simplest statements in the *protocol-language* refer to the given, and describe directly given experience or phenomena, i.e. the simplest states of which knowledge may be had. The elements that are directly given are the simplest sensations and feelings.'

[1] Op. cit., p. 42.

The explanation of Carnap's allowing himself to talk in this way is quite simple; he maintains that he is talking in the material mode of speech. He claims that though in appearance talking of the relation of language to the world he is really only talking about language. To make this clear he offers translations of some of the most difficult remarks in the formal mode. Thus he translates the last quotation we made from him as follows: 'The simplest statements in the *protocol-language* are protocol-statements, i.e. statements needing no justification and serving as foundation for all the remaining statements of science. Protocol statements are of the same kind as: "joy now", "here, now, blue", "there, red".'

At first sight this does not look too unreasonable, but we must look closer. When he says 'Protocol statements are of the same kind as: "joy now", "here, now, blue", "there, red" ', Carnap means, or ought to mean, that all protocol sentences are of the same syntactical type as 'joy, now' and the rest. He does not mean, officially at any rate, statements which as directly report reality as does 'joy, now', but statements to which the same rules for the formation of sentences and their transformation into others apply. Bearing this in mind, we ought immediately to ask two obvious questions: Why does Carnap choose sentences of this syntactical form rather than any others to fulfil this particular basic role in language? And on what principles does one decide which of these protocols of the right syntactical form to accept and which to reject? Carnap cannot give the obvious answers because statements of this syntactical form are the kind which we use to report experience; and we select those for acceptance which do as a matter of fact record experience accurately. For according to Carnap to say that a statement is of the kind which reports experience is just to say, in the material mode, that it is of this syntactical form.

The well-nigh incredible answers in fact given are these. It is purely a matter of convention that we select sentences of this syntactical form as the basic protocol statements; and we accept those protocols which are accepted by the accredited scientists and reject those which are not. Carnap says, for example,[1] 'Every concrete proposition belonging to the physicalist language-system can in suitable circumstances serve as a protocol proposition'. We could go on now to ask why we accept the protocols of accredited scientists, why they are accredited, and how we know within syntax that these or those are accepted by accredited scientists. But it is clearly not worth while to pursue this theory further. Philosophy cannot just be logical syntax, nor can a language be characterized by a vocabulary understood as a list of marks on paper with formation and transformation rules. Carnap and his fellows probably did as well as can be done by this thesis. But it is impossible; they could only make it appear plausible by relying on the natural meaning of what was supposed to be merely syntax in the material mode of speech. Carnap, of course, came to see this. He now acknowledges, and writes on, a branch of philosophy which he calls semantics and which deals with this forbidden topic of the relation of words to things. But on the credit side of the Carnap of other days it must be said that he was one of the few in the period of classical logical empiricism who honestly faced the need to maintain consistently that philosophy consisted solely of tautological transformations, of analytical equivalences. But for his errors the need for some revision of the doctrine would not have been seen so quickly.

The reader may very well wonder why to say that a statement is to be accepted because it records a fact was regarded as such a dangerous thing, and why it was regarded as metaphysical. For it does not seem very similar to the more grandiose statements of speculative metaphysics. So far as Wittgenstein himself was concerned the matter is not so hard

[1] '*Über Protokollsätze*', quoted by Ayer in 'Verification and Experience', p. 145.

to understand. For (1) when Wittgenstein talked about a proposition picturing a fact he was certainly talking metaphysics, and intentionally. For this sort of fact was not just any fact but a very metaphysical variety. As Wittgenstein used the word it was probably not a fact that Queen Anne is dead, since Queen Anne was probably, like the rest of us, a logical construction, and not a genuine object or particular. One must be talking metaphysics whatever one says about this sort of fact. (2) If Wittgenstein's doctrine that a proposition is a picture of a fact is accepted, then it seems plain that one cannot talk about the relation of language to fact without violation of syntax; for one cannot produce a picture of the relation of a picture to what is pictured, the fact. This relation must show itself, and what is shown cannot be said. It seems that later logical positivists partly thought that all talk about facts must be as metaphysical as Wittgenstein's and partly accepted the consequences of the 'picture' theory of language from Wittgenstein somewhat uncritically even when they had abandoned the theory of language itself.

Probably, however, some more general, *a priori*, considerations played a great part. For example, the dichotomy 'tautological–empirical' seemed to be exhaustive to the positivists, and anything which could not be brought into these two categories was rejected as metaphysical. But philosophy had to be logical rather than empirical—one cannot carry on empirical studies in an arm-chair—and a logical inquiry is concerned, it seems, with statements and their relations to each other, not with the relation of language to fact. To some logical empiricists it seemed more tolerable to abandon, or to treat as in the material mode of speech, such statements as apparently involved extra-logical excursions than to allow any exception to the fundamental dichotomy 'logical–empirical'.

Our sketch of the salient features of logical empiricism, in its confident youth, and of the account it gave of the nature and point of analysis is now complete, though we shall have occasion later to consider some of the logical empiricists' views on some more detailed topics. We have not examined, and cannot examine, the contribution they made to many detailed problems which fall outside our main inquiry.

The two points that I have tried hardest to bring out about logical empiricism have been these: (1) while abandoning the metaphysics of logical atomism, at least officially and in intention, the logical empiricists retained substantially the same view of the scope and nature of analysis; but it was now conceived as revealing the logical structure of the language of science, of informative discourse, not of the facts with which science deals. Roughly the same propositions remained basic under both dispensations, whether they were said to picture facts or not, and roughly the same things remained as logical constructions. (2) The positivists all claimed that the sole legitimate propositions of philosophy were tautologies—verbal equivalences (Ayer, indeed, adds that empirical statements about the history of philosophy may be called philosophical, but this makes no real difference). Some maintained this thesis with considerable consistency but at the expense of intolerable paradox—for example, Carnap and the radical physicalists; others were more plausible but less consistent. Thus much of the criticism of Carnap which we have reproduced here is derived from the writings of Ayer, who maintained that we must be allowed to talk about the agreement of propositions with reality. Yet this is quite impossible on the general account of the nature of philosophy given by Ayer in *Language Truth and Logic*, where he maintains that, apart from history of philosophy, all philosophical statements must be tautological equivalences. Whatever defect we may find in these and other doctrines of the logical empiricists, their services in arousing philosophy from dogmatic slumbers and in making philosophers look really carefully at such problems as the nature of metaphysics and significance cannot be over-estimated. 'Classical' logical positivism may be dead, but it did not live in vain.

It will be recalled that we considered that logical atomism came to be abandoned for two reasons; the first was the general rejection of metaphysics, including *a fortiori* logical atomism, the second that on examination a number of flaws were discovered in the metaphysics of atomism which made it less attractive as metaphysics. We have now examined in some detail the first of these reasons, and the consequential change of attitude towards analysis. We must now turn to examine the more detailed objections to the metaphysics. We cannot possibly discuss them all or go into them fully, but we must look at some of the more important ones, saving the most important, from our point of view, to the last. These more detailed flaws which were found in logical atomism undoubtedly led to a speedier and wider acceptance of logical positivism than would otherwise have occurred. Many who accepted it would have at least hesitated longer if, as metaphysics, logical atomism had appeared impeccable.

9

SOME DETAILED DEFECTS IN LOGICAL ATOMISM

A. THE ONE PERFECT LANGUAGE

IT will be recalled that the metaphysics of logical atomism is, in effect, an account of what the structure of the world must be, granted that the symbolic calculus of *Principia Mathematica*, the great logical system of Whitehead and Russell, can be regarded as in principle, if not in every detail, as the skeleton of the one perfect language, lacking only the flesh constituted by a vocabulary, a perfect language into which ordinary language could be translated since it differed only in doing the same kind of thing in a less clear, efficient, and explicit way. But if the language of *Principia Mathematica* were found to fulfil a quite different task from ordinary language, so that the two were not, even in principle, inter-translatable; or if other calculi could be found which as calculi seemed to be quite as correctly formed as that of *Principia Mathematica;* then it would be hard to find any justification for regarding that calculus as the skeleton of the perfect language, and in consequence it would be hard to justify any inference from the structure of that calculus to the structure of the universe. There would be no reason, without a further, not very obvious, argument, to believe that the universe mirrored this rather than some other calculus or natural language. Difficulties were raised on both these scores.

(1) *Alternative calculi*

Those philosophers who found little or no difficulty in regarding calculi as skeletons of potential languages were much struck by the fertile invention of new calculi in this period. Apart from the discovery of the more exotic three- and n-valued calculi by the Polish logicians, Carnap and others found it possible to construct many different calculi containing more or less, and even different, operators. There seemed to be as much ground for supposing some of these calculi to be language-skeletons as for so regarding *Principia Mathematica*. Consequently these philosophers, who included most of the Vienna Circle, abandoned the notion of the perfect language. This was naturally a reason for abandoning the metaphysics of logical atomism; it was also natural for them to conclude that analysis was of language only, and that from the structure of a language revealed by analysis nothing could be inferred about anything else.

(2) *Ordinary language and the calculus of* Principia Mathematica

But British philosophers, who, under the influence of Moore, were largely interested in the analysis of common-sense beliefs as expressed in common-sense language, were more influenced by the difficulty of regarding ordinary language as having the structure of the formulae of *Principia*. For example, the language of *Principia* is in general a language of explicit truth-functions, i.e. it is extensional, though, as we have already seen, there are difficulties about generality, e.g. about regarding $(x).\phi x$ as a truth-function of ϕa, ϕb, . . ., ϕn. . . . This being so, it was necessary for the logical atomists to maintain that ordinary language was implicitly truth-functional; indeed, one of the main objects of the analysis of ordinary statements was to make these truth-functions explicit.

We need not treat further the difficulty about generality; this raised the problem whether either the perfect language or ordinary language was wholly composed of truth-functions; it worried atomists, but we need not say more on that point.

But another difficulty arose, which was whether ordinary language was truth-functional in cases where the only possible translation into the language of *Principia* was quite clearly so by general agreement.

We must avoid here the technical, and tangled, controversies regarding the paradoxes of material implication. We can sufficiently illustrate the great difficulty of translating the statements of ordinary language about entailments or implications into the language of *Principia* without entangling ourselves in that thicket. When we make a statement of entailment, say that an object's being coloured entails its being extended, or that the axioms of Euclid entail his theorems, we are not merely saying that it is not the case that the entailing proposition is false and the entailed proposition true, but saying that the truth of the entailed proposition can be inferred from the truth of the other without independent knowledge of the truth of the entailed proposition. Now it was generally agreed that the nearest that the truth-functional language could get to 'p entails q' was 'not p without q', the truth-function which is true for all values of p and q except when p is false and q is true. This truth-function 'not p without q' was often read 'p materially implies q' on account of this supposed analogy. But apart from the difficulty of regarding implication as a sentence connective of the same kind as 'and', 'or', and even 'if . . . then', it is clear that there may be 'material implication' between two statements when the second cannot be inferred from the first. For example, that London is north of Edinburgh materially implies that water is a liquid, since it is not the case that the first proposition is true and the second false; but one cannot infer one from the other. Given that 'p materially implies q' is a tautology, we can no doubt infer that q given that p; but it is hard to see how the whole statement ' "p materially implies q" is a tautology' is itself truth-functional. Wittgenstein foresaw this difficulty; he maintained that when 'p materially implies q' is a tautology, that shows itself and it is illegitimate to say it, though of course when it shows itself we can infer q from p. This amounts to prohibiting the use of such sentences as 'p entails q'; few philosophers were prepared to accept such a prohibition.[1]

Thus 'p entails q' seemed to resist a truth-functional interpretation; 'If p then q' shares some at least of the difficulties, since p seems to be put forward as a ground for q. Unfulfilled conditionals, of the form 'If A had been B then C would have been D' seemed especially difficult, and ingenious but unconvincing attempts to translate them into more and more complicated truth-functions cropped up at frequent intervals over a long period in philosophical periodicals; they are still not unknown. These examples illustrate sufficiently one sort of difficulty which was found in regarding ordinary language as translatable into the language of *Principia Mathematica*. The reader who wishes to go further into this sort of difficulty can safely be referred to Strawson's *Introduction to Logical Theory*.[2]

Another type of proposition which seemed to present crucial difficulties for the truth-functional interpretation of ordinary language was that of which 'Jones believes that p' and 'Smith observes that q' are typical examples. The proposition 'Jones believes that p' seems to be complex and to contain p as an element; but it is not a truth-function of p since the question whether Jones believes that p is not settled at all by finding out whether p is true. Once again Wittgenstein anticipated this difficulty and tried to resolve it in a passage of almost impenetrable obscurity.[3] Interpretations differ even among close students of Wittgenstein, but he appears to assimilate belief to the uttering of a sentence, so that Jones's belief *is* the set of words he utters and 'Jones believes that p' can therefore be said to be of the form " 'p' says p"; here the sentence 'p'

---

[1] See the *Tractatus Logico-Philosophicus*, especially 5.131, 5.525, 6.127.
[2] See especially Ch. III, Part II.   [3] *Tractatus*, 5.54–5.5422.

is in the first instance mentioned not used. But his resolution of this difficulty was not understood fully, and in so far as it was understood it was not accepted.

Thus in the discovery of new logical calculi and in the discovery of comparatively simple statements of ordinary language which resisted a truth-functional interpretation we have two grounds for doubting whether the calculus of *Principia* had any right to be regarded as the one and only skeleton of a perfect language, and even whether it could be satisfactorily clothed in the vocabulary of existing languages. The claim that analysis of statements into its forms would reveal the structure of the world had therefore to be looked upon with the greatest suspicion. Logical positivism was free from at least this sort of difficulty.

B. SOLIPSISM

Another objection to the specific doctrines of logical atomism was that when combined, as it usually was, with a fairly advanced empiricism it seemed to lead inevitably to solipsism, and by an even shorter route than the well-trodden paths of traditional empiricism. We have seen that the atomic propositions from which all others are derived as truth-functions of them may contain, apart from names of qualities and relations, only logically proper names of the constituents of the facts depicted, and no descriptions. If a description is used instead of a purely demonstrative symbol, then by the theory of descriptions a general proposition is produced, not a picture of a single atomic fact. Further a logically proper name can be given only to an object of acquaintance while one is actually acquainted with it; one cannot use a demonstrative symbol to name a thing which is not present. Now it was unquestioned by almost everybody, during the whole period with which we are concerned, that the only objects of acquaintance, or at least the only particular objects of acquaintance, are sense-date. But sense-data are essentially private to the person who has them, and hence it follows that no two people can ever both be acquainted with the same object. Russell saw this quite clearly, and therefore he said in the second of his *Monist* lectures on the philosophy of logical atomism in 1918:

One can use 'this' as a name to stand for a particular with which one is acquainted at the moment. We say 'This is white'. If you agree that 'This is white', meaning the this that you see, you are using 'this' as a proper name. But if you try to apprehend the proposition that I am expressing when I say 'This is white', you cannot do it. If you mean this piece of chalk as a physical object, then you are not using a proper name.

So not only are we in the usual empiricist difficulty of inferring our friends from our sense-data—of finding propositions which both are truth-functions of propositions about our sense-data and refer to the experiences of others, but the totality of atomic propositions intelligible to me, and hence of all propositions intelligible to me, is intelligible to no one else. Any communication is therefore theoretically impossible.

Thus the world is the totality of facts. The world is given for me by the totality of my atomic propositions. There is nothing else. Russell did not draw and accept this grim conclusion. But Wittgenstein, whom we have already found anticipating the difficulties which were later to be generally felt, had seen all this from the first. He said:

5.62   In fact what solipsism *intends* is quite correct, only it cannot be *said*, but it shows itself. That the world is *my* world shows itself in the fact that the limits of language (*the* language, which I alone understand) means the limits of my world.

5.621   The world and life are one.

5.63   I am my world (the microcosm).

It is true that Wittgenstein went on:

5.631   The thinking, presenting subject; there is no such thing.

5.64   Here we see that solipsism strictly carried out coincides

with pure realism. The I in solipsism shrinks to an exten-
sionless point and there remains the reality co-ordinated
with it.

But this appears to be the cold comfort of being consoled for
having no friends by the fact that I have no transcendental
ego either.

At first people neither understood Wittgenstein very well
nor saw how hard it would be to eliminate the solipsistic
element from atomism. But they came to be more and more
worried by it. In a theoretical way, solipsism was a live issue
at this period. It will therefore be instructive, if not quite in
place here, to consider what alternative logical positivism had
to offer.

The task of the logical positivist was to show that statements about other people could be analysed in such a way
that they would be verifiable to the person considering the
statement, and so significant to him. Since most of them
regarded the basic protocol as being about the sense-contents
or sense-data of the individual, this meant that verification
must ultimately be in terms of one's own sense-contents.
Adopting this line Ayer tackled the problem as follows:[1]

Just as I must define material things and my own self in terms
of their empirical manifestations, so I must define other people in
terms of their empirical manifestations—that is, in terms of the
behaviour of their bodies, and ultimately in terms of sense-contents. The assumption that 'behind' these sense-contents there
are entities which are not even in principle accessible to my
observation can have no more significance for me than the admittedly metaphysical assumption that such entities 'underlie' the
sense-contents which constitute material things for me, or my own
self. And thus I find that I have as good a reason to believe in the
existence of other people as I have to believe in the existence of

[1] *Language Truth and Logic*, p. 130. A less drastic position later adopted
by Ayer is to be found in his *Foundations of Empirical Knowledge*, pp. 168–
70. But this later position requires an important modification of the
verification principle.

material things. For in each case my hypothesis is verified by the occurrence in my sense-history of the appropriate series of sense-contents.

Ayer adds that by this analysis he does not deny the consciousness of others, 'for when I assert that an object is conscious I am asserting no more than that it would, in response to any conceivable test, exhibit the empirical manifestations of consciousness'.

To one who does not accept Ayer's basic position this may appear to be merely bold, brash Humpty-Dumptyism with language, in which words are paid extra to give an appearance of reasonableness to a position which is really identical with the solipsism which is supposed to be repudiated. But there is a crucial difference from the solipsism forced on the logical atomists; for them the existence of the experiences of others 'behind' the sense-contents was a significant problem. This problem was now banished as unreal and metaphysical, which permitted the worried to banish it from their minds; this gave a real attraction to the position adopted by Ayer for those who saw no other consistent alternative save metaphysical solipsism, which admitted to denying what, if significant, it would be absurd to deny.

Neurath, maintaining as he did that references to experience are really syntactical and that the choice of primitive protocol was conventional, had another device for dealing with solipsism. If we adopt as primitive protocol such sentences as 'Otto's protocol: "Red, now"', and 'Rudolf's protocol: "Joy, now"', then for Neurath to say that Carnap had experiences was nothing more than to say that 'Rudolf's protocol: "Joy, now" ' was an accepted sentence. But we have already seen that to gain this advantage Neurath had to go a long way down a road where few would wish to follow him.

So much for the solipsistic dangers of logical atomism and the heroic surgery by means of which the logical positivists eliminated them.

C. ATOMIC PROPOSITIONS

The conception of an atomic proposition is plainly a difficult one. The atomists had committed themselves to saying that such a proposition would contain only logically proper names of particulars—ultimate particulars, and possibly names of components, suitably ordered, but they had been very reluctant to attempt to give an example of one. Wisdom indeed, it will be remembered, had doubted whether anyone could ever give an actual example of one. For he suspected that 'this' was always a concealed description, equivalent to, say, 'the thing I am pointing to' and that words like 'red' always referred to a range of colour and not to a perfectly determinate shade. In either case an element of generality would have entered the proposition, and hence it would not be atomic.

That problem was much debated, but even if we suppress these doubts of Wisdom there are other perplexing issues. Not least striking is the odd uninformative character to which the atomic proposition was supposed to conform. This can be illustrated by a well-known and amusing translation of Wisdom's. Making up new logically proper names 'thet' and 'thot' to eke out the slender existing supply, he translates the sentence 'The son of the brother of the mother of the boy kissed the girl with the almond eyes' first of all to read: 'This is the son of thet, and thet is the mother of thot, and thot is a boy, and this kissed Sylvia.' 'This sentence nearly pictures a fact', added Wisdom, 'and if we eliminate words which merely emphasize spatial order and write "This son that, and that brother thet, and thet mother thot, and thot boy, and this kissed Sylvia", we have a sentence which pictures a fact.' The difficulty is to know what to do with it when one has got it, especially as we must remember that sentences containing logically proper names are, as Russell himself insisted, intelligible only to the speaker, and presumably to him only while the objects named continue to be for him objects of acquaintance. Also Sylvia, the boy, and all his family are presumably really logical constructions.

Yet in spite of its oddity, substantially this view of basic propositions was held even by some who were not logical atomists and who did not uphold it on the ground that only propositions of this sort, however useless in conversation, were the only ones which exhibited accurately the structure of fact. For it had other attractions; in particular it seemed the goal in the quest for certainty. Philosophers have always sought to find some absolutely indubitable truths as a basis of knowledge; empiricists have been liable to think that such a goal must be attainable, if anywhere, in reports of direct experience which were free from all elements of dubious interpretation or extrapolation. The use of logically proper names seemed to many to be the way to secure such plain, ungarnished reports, and thus to achieve the certainty of incorrigible propositions. It was thought that if all the names in propositions were logically proper names then they would have to refer to what is actually experienced, since one cannot use a logically proper name of anything which is not present as an object of acquaintance; and as there is no descriptive element in logically proper names we are guaranteed against the possibility of misdescription. The danger, however, was clearly that in ensuring that one said nothing which might be erroneous one might be too cautious and say nothing at all.

Ayer attacked this conception on such lines, arguing as follows:[1]

What we cannot admit is that any synthetic proposition can be purely ostensive. For the notion of an ostensive proposition appears to involve a contradiction in terms. It implies that there could be a sentence which consisted of purely demonstrative symbols and was at the same time intelligible. And this is not even

---

[1] *Language Truth and Logic*, p. 91. The whole argument of pp. 90–94 is relevant and rewarding.

a logical possibility. A sentence which consisted of demonstrative symbols would not express a genuine proposition. It would be a mere ejaculation, in no way characterizing that to which it was supposed to refer.

The fact is that one cannot in language point to an object without describing it. If a sentence is to express a proposition, it cannot merely name a situation; it must say something about it. And in describing a situation one is not merely 'registering' a sense-content; one is classifying it in some way or other, and that means going beyond what is immediately given. But a proposition would be ostensive only if it recorded what was immediately experienced, without referring in any way beyond. And as this is not possible, it follows that no genuine synthetic proposition can be ostensive, and consequently that none can be absolutely certain.

Accordingly we hold not merely that no ostensive propositions ever are expressed, but that it is inconceivable that any ostensive proposition ever should be expressed.

Later, as Ayer reports in his 'Verification and Experience', Moore persuaded him that the only possible kind of error in basic propositions is linguistic error. Here, I think, first thoughts were best. If a person says 'This is red' he is not merely liable to use the wrong word (having meant, say, green), he is liable to have classified the thing in question wrongly. If he is not using the word 'red' in a way which involves classification, it is hard to see that he is saying anything, however uninformative. But this is still a live issue; the argument continues. We, however, are not now concerned to solve the problem, but only to note that some philosophers came to doubt, for the sort of reason given by Ayer, whether the sort of proposition which was regarded as fundamental by the logical atomists was even a possibility. To them it seemed that the only way to avoid all risk of error was to say nothing.[1]

[1] Readers who wish to follow up this question would be well advised to read the relevant portions of Austin's 'Other Minds', *Proceedings of the Aristotelian Society*, supplementary volume, 1946, reprinted in *Logic and Language*, vol. ii, ed. Flew. Also see Ayer, 'Basic Propositions', *Methods of Analysis*, ed. Black. There is a vast literature in periodicals.

D. PICTURING FACTS

Classical atomism, as part of its doctrine of the one perfect language, had maintained that the relation between a proposition and the fact it stated was one of picturing; there must be structural similarity between a proposition and the fact it represents, however much this may be concealed by the conventions of the language, and therefore there is only one sort of language possible, of which natural languages are stylistic variants. So far as Wittgenstein was concerned this criticism was sometimes somewhat off the mark since his critics, like some of his followers, misunderstood him and thought that by a picture he meant something which looked like the original. As we have seen, Wittgenstein did not hold this view, and even maintained that a gramophone record was in his sense a picture of a score. But the criticism was very cogent against some of the other logical atomists, and in any case what is important in the history of this period is the accepted interpretation of Wittgenstein. Further, Wittgenstein, even correctly interpreted, was not wholly immune from the criticism.

A fairly early, and usefully succinct, statement of the basic difficulty in the doctrine was made by Ryle:[1]

I cannot myself credit what seems to be the doctrine of Wittgenstein and the school of logical grammarians who owe allegiance to him, that what makes an expression formally proper to a fact is some real and non-conventional one-one picturing relation between the composition of the expression and that of the fact. For I do not see how a fact or state of affairs can be deemed like or even unlike in structure a sentence, gesture or diagram. For a fact is not a collection—even an arranged collection—of bits in the way in which a sentence is an arranged collection of noises or a map an arranged collection of scratches.

[1] 'Systematically Misleading Expressions', *Proceedings of the Aristotelian Society*, 1931–2, reprinted in *Logic and Language*, vol. i, ed. Flew.

Ryle goes on to say:

On the other hand it is not easy to accept what seems to be the alternative that it is just by convention that a given grammatical form is specially dedicated to facts of a given logical form. . . . It is, however, my present view that the propriety of grammatical to logical form is more nearly conventional than natural.

A time was to come when Ryle's statement that one cannot compare the structure of language and fact would be taken more seriously than he then saw his way to take it and the attempt to talk about the logical structure of facts would be abandoned.

It is interesting to compare and contrast this argument of Ryle's with a rather later attack on the doctrine of picturing made by Ayer. He said:[1]

It is sometimes suggested that this relation of agreement is of same kind as that which holds between a picture and that of which it is a picture. I do not think that this is true. It is possible indeed to construct picture-languages; no doubt they have their advantages; but it surely cannot be maintained that they alone are legitimate; or that a language such as English is really a picture-language although we do not know it. But if English is not a picture-language and propositions expressed in English are sometimes verified, as they surely are, then it cannot be the case that this relation of agreement with which we are concerned is one of picturing. Besides there is this further difficulty. If any propositions are pictures, presumably false propositions are as well as true ones. In other words, we cannot tell from the form of the proposition, that is, merely by looking at the picture, whether it depicts a real situation or not. But how then are we to distinguish the true picture from the false? Must we not say that the true picture agrees with reality whereas the false one does not? But in that case the introduction of the notion of picturing does not serve our purpose. It does not enable us to dispense with the notion of agreement.

Ayer goes on to say: 'The same objections hold against

[1] 'Verification and Experience', *Proceedings of the Aristotelian Society*, 1936–7; a similar argument is to be found in his *Foundations of Empirical Knowledge*, p. 106.

those who say that this relation of agreement is one of identity of structure. This is to treat propositions as if they were maps.' Once again he maintains that we might construct a language like this, but as we also need not, the identity of structure cannot be the important thing. He says:

If I am speaking English I may use the words 'I am angry' to say that I am angry. You may say, if you like, that in doing so I am obeying a meaning rule of the English language. For this to be possible it is not the least necessary that my words should in any way resemble the state of anger which they describe. That 'this is red' is used to say that this is red does not imply that it bears any relation of resemblance, whether of structure or content, to an actual or hypothetical red patch.

Ayer's final statement of the point is excellent. He sees clearly that it is the established use of a statement alone which determines what it can be used to communicate, and that some appropriateness of structure of a logical kind, which Ryle still hankers after, is beside the point. On the other hand, whereas Ryle had maintained that it was a mistake in principle to require identity of structure between statement and fact stated on the ground that a statement cannot be like or unlike the fact it states, Ayer has argued that structural resemblance or identity may hold between a language (e.g. a pictorial language) and fact, but need not. What the atomists had declared essential and Ryle had declared impossible Ayer now holds to be possible but unnecessary. Here, I think that Ayer has betrayed an important misunderstanding of the doctrine of picturing which it is important to clear up.

A warning that this is a misconception might have been given by the express claim of Wittgenstein that a proposition of ordinary language need not, and clearly does not, have a superficial resemblance to fact, and yet is in his sense a picture, and still more clearly by his comparison of the relation of language to fact both to the relation of a map to the earth's surface and also to the relation of waves of sound to a gramophone record, superficially very different, without wishing to identify it with either. What Ayer says of picture- and map-languages is only true if we are thinking of the historical genesis of language rather than its logical character. Not every picture, in the ordinary sense, is a means of communication, and that shows that by merely being a picture in the ordinary sense nothing can have a meaning; something more must be necessary, even if it is natural to make use of pictures. There are no picture-languages, if it is meant that the language has meaning simply in virtue of its pictorial character, and Wittgenstein was not suggesting that any language was pictorial in this sense. So that when Ayer says that only some languages are pictorial, not all, as the position attacked maintained, he was arguing incorrectly; for the sense in which some languages are picture-languages and others are not is irrelevant to the point at issue. Arguing as he does, it is not surprising that he finds a logical relation of agreement necessary in addition to the natural pictorial similarity; but the pictorial relation of the atomists was meant to be a more explicit version of this relation of agreement, not a mere natural similarity. The better criticism is what Ayer's last quoted remarks imply, and Ryle expressly said, that the notion of picturing and structural similarity has no part to play in the explanation of language at all.

Summing up, we may say that the basic objection to the doctrine of picturing at this period was that the 'picturing' theory at least underestimated the conventional character of linguistic forms; it implied, wrongly, that there was a natural appropriateness of some linguistic forms, some structural likeness of language and fact. There was as yet no general awareness of further difficulties which would soon be raised. We need not go fully into these, but a hint of them will not lead too far afield. First, is it always right to say that an ordinary indicative statement refers, whether by picturing or otherwise, to a fact? Secondly, is it clear what is meant by talking of the form, logical or otherwise, of a fact? Is there not some danger that in doing so we are reading into the fact what is to be found in the language we use? Thirdly, are we right in supposing that we find the world ready divided into a number of facts, each self-contained and waiting for its logical snap-shot to be taken? Might not the number of separate facts to be found in some matter depend at least partly on the way we look at it? We do not need to ban talk about facts as metaphysical, as the physicalists did, but we need to be aware that it is not so simple a concept as it appears to be in its four-lettered innocence. Wisdom said that in his articles on logical constructions he would use the word 'fact' as it was used in the *Strand Magazine*; but it needs closer scrutiny than that.[1]

Those four difficulties, the notion of the one perfect extensional language, solipsism, basic propositions, and the doctrine of picturing, are among the chief difficulties which were already noticed in logical atomism when logical positivism was widening its hold in England in the early and middle thirties. Some were difficulties solely for atomism, or mainly so; others, such as solipsism were difficulties for logical positivism also, but it was thought, or hoped, that they could be evaded. But a little later another, more formidable, difficulty began to be noticed, a difficulty for atomism, logical positivism, and all the many compromises between them. It was perhaps rather obscurely recognized by most philosophers; the complete diagnosis was only possible in the light of the radically different view of philosophy, analysis, and language which was soon to be put forward. At present we shall represent it merely as an endemic disease in analysis, avoiding any forward-looking diagnosis. But it deserves a separate chapter.

---

[1] Some amplification of these obscure hints will be found in Waismann's paper 'Verifiability', *Proceedings of the Aristotelian Society*, supplementary volume, 1945, reprinted in *Language and Logic*, vol. i, ed. Flew. See especially Part III.

10

THE IMPOSSIBILITY OF REDUCTIVE ANALYSIS

WE must now turn to the most serious difficulty of all, the one which seemed to render pointless the whole metaphysics of logical atomism and most conclusively altered the whole course of philosophy. This difficulty gradually forced itself on the attention of philosophers at a rather later date than those which we have just considered, so it will be convenient to start with a sketch of the situation as it was in advanced analytic circles in the years from about 1935 until 1938.

On the whole the anti-metaphysical position that any metaphysics was nonsense was accepted, in spite of the difficulties which we have mentioned and of which philosophers were more or less aware—such difficulties as that it was hard to avoid altogether talk about the relation of language to fact, which was metaphysical according to a strict interpretation of the positivist doctrine of the nature of philosophy. But the general conception of the nature of the job to be done had not changed much from that proclaimed by Russell in the early days of logical atomism, even if the justification of it had. One still represented language as analysable into basic propositions, even if one no longer spoke of revealing the structure of facts but rather of showing the structure of the language of science and common sense by analysing its propositions into more basic ones which could be directly verified and which were therefore the ultimate meaning of these other propositions. This was so even if a less stringent and more relativistic view of the nature of basic propositions was prevalent than in the hey-day of logical atomism. Still, therefore, the old debates about the analysis of, for example, material object statements into statements about sense-data went on as before. It can hardly be over-emphasized that the vast majority of philosophers in England at this time had no serious doubt that such analysis was the main business of philosophy, whatever difficulties of comparative detail might vex them. The anti-metaphysical verification principle chiefly had the effect, for the more advanced analysts who accepted it, of an *a priori* guarantee that some phenomenalistic analysis would do—there could be no significant analysis that went beyond the sense-data to physical occupants and the like, as some more moderate analysts, such as H. H. Price in his *Perception*, had claimed.

It is true that many of the objections to the classical doctrines of logical atomism, some of which we have considered, were as much of an embarrassment to the new form of the analytic enterprise as to the old. For the extensionalist view of language was still widely accepted, if not with thorough consistency—language must be of a truth-functional character if it is to be analysed down into basic propositions. There must be no ultimate complex propositions. Yet, as we have seen, difficulties were beginning to be noticed in this doctrine. Solipsism, too, was as inescapable a difficulty for positivism as it had been for logical atomism, though the anti-metaphysical dogma had changed the form of the discussion. Consequently, though philosophers sometimes could drown their worries in an orgy of anti-metaphysical destruction, they were still there. But, as usual, the objectors to analytic philosophy, who would gladly have kept these difficulties in the foreground, were mostly too ignorant of the precise doctrines of their opponents to put their objections in a form which could have much effect on them, so that they could fairly easily forget their troubles when they wished; the difficulties which we have so far noticed were treated as minor embarrassments and the attempts at analysis continued. Once again the final dissolution was to come from within in its own good time.

In treating these difficulties as minor embarrassments the analysts were not being so unreasonable. We must never forget that logical atomism and logical positivism were not simply doctrines held for their own sake. Both flourished as justifications of the reductive analysis which had always seemed to be the main task of the empiricist, even if the form of the justification had an effect on the exact way in which the analysis was described and carried on. The most important task of the verification principle was to guarantee that empiricist analysis was possible, though it also had the effect of eliminating some other forms of philosophical inquiry. As long, therefore, as analysts felt happy deep down about the general satisfactoriness of reductive analysis as the task of philosophers, so long any inadequacy in its current justification was a fairly minor matter. We may remember, for example, that there were endemic difficulties about the exact formulation of the verification principle so that it would exclude all that was required and no more. This problem was never solved, but it did not really worry philosophers who accepted it. It did not make them wonder whether their whole method of philosophizing was perhaps wrong. The really serious thing would be a ground for doubting the propriety of reductive analysis itself, not one for doubting a detail of its current justification.[1]

And now we come to the big trouble, a trouble for logical atomism and logical positivism alike, and also for all the more or less eclectic and intermediate positions held by more cautious analysts. For unlike our other difficulties it is a direct difficulty about the fundamental possibility of reductive analysis. It was first fully recognized in Cambridge under the stimulus of Wittgenstein in his new phase, after he returned to philosophy in 1929; the first explicit statement of it is to be

[1] This is part of the explanation of how so conservative a philosopher as Moore could be regarded as an ally and mentor by such radicals as Ayer. He, like them, was an analyst in his practice, whatever else they disagreed about.

found in Wisdom's 'Metaphysics and Verification'.[1] But it also forced itself on philosophers' attention as a more or less empirical difficulty—nobody was producing any satisfactory analyses. We must look into the history of this.

The analytic movement had had its impulse, as we have seen from Russell's logical and mathematical researches; it was, said Russell, 'a kind of logical doctrine which seems to me to result from the philosophy of mathematics'.[2] We may recall that Descartes, too, based his methods and doctrines on his mathematical successes. Now something like reductive analysis had worked very well in logic and mathematics on the whole. It was clearly possible to treat rational numbers as logical constructions out of natural numbers in pure mathematics, and irrationals as logical constructions out of rationals; the job had been done. In logic, classes could be treated as logical constructions out of propositional functions. In logic even the integers with which the pure mathematician started could be eliminated. As a rough indication of how this was done we may quote Russell's translation of 'Not three people are interested in mathematical logic' into 'If x is interested in mathematical logic, and y is interested and z is interested, then $x = y$ or $y = z$ or $x = z$'. The word 'three' has gone in favour of logical variables. In addition there was the logical analysis of descriptions, which had not only proved itself in mathematical logic but seemed capable of eliminating for ever at one stroke all the Meinongian realms of being.

What Russell had done with such success so quickly in mathematical logic had now to be done in other spheres. It was true that attempts to do this in other spheres had been made before, but without conspicuous success; nobody could think that Berkeley's 'There is a table here, that is I see it' would do as it stood. But then people had very often failed in

[1] *Mind*, 1938.
[2] *The Philosophy of Logical Atomism*, p. 1.

spheres where Russell had now succeeded. Now Russell had provided the paradigms of success for all to imitate, and had provided the technique and the skeleton of a perfect language, the language of *Principia Mathematica*, in which to do it. Thus after a long period of eclipse the traditional reductive analysis of British empiricism was taken up again in a fine fever of enthusiasm.

But what sure successes were achieved in the field of new-level, or reductive, analysis, outside the province of mathematical logic? Wisdom had, indeed, analysed the llama in terms of (ordinary) llamas, and, for good measure, the average plumber in terms of (ordinary) plumbers. But in neither case was this getting down to rock bottom, for it was generally agreed that both llamas and plumbers, even ordinary ones, were themselves logical constructions. Fictional entities also were analysed away in terms of sentences in books, the words of tale-tellers, and the like, though not in quite so convincing a way. As Wisdom himself later put it: 'The extra entities in the universe of discourse all went up in smoke, though from the fictional entities there lingered still a peculiar smell.'[1] Though these analyses never got to anything like atomic propositions, they were at least fairly successful so far as they went. These were the examples of successful analysis which were always given, and consequently the ones given here. But these are after all small game. The bigger game were nations—perhaps still only middle-sized game; these were logical constructions out of people, as all confidently agreed. The really big game were things and people, which were, in the eyes of the cautious, probably, and in the eyes of the more sanguine, certainly, logical constructions out of sense-data and/or events. But in spite of this *a priori* agreement about the general nature of the analysis nobody actually succeeded in analysing nations into people or people into events or sense-data. We will start with nations, as supposedly one of

[1] 'Metaphysics and Verification', *Mind*, 1938, p. 460.

the easiest and most certain examples, in order to discover where the difficulty in carrying out the analysis arose.

Nations, the doctrine ran, were logical constructions out of people; England and France were logical constructions, for example, out of their nationals. Another way of putting this is to say that statements about England and France can be analysed in terms of people, or, more exactly, that statements containing the words 'England' and 'France' can be replaced by statements in which they and their synonyms (such as 'Perfidious Albion') do not appear, but names of people and descriptions of people do appear. 'England' is an incomplete symbol. In each case the analysis is to have the same meaning as the analysandum. Let us then take a simple statement about England and attempt the analysis. The statement 'England declared war in 1939' will do as well as any. This is clearly not equivalent to 'All Englishmen declared war in 1939'. A number even of the Englishmen most active in the prosecution of the war had no part in its declaration. Clearly, too, an enumeration of what every Englishman did in 1939 is not required. Nobody needs to know what I for one did on even the 3rd of September in order to know the meaning of the analysandum. Let us try 'The Foreign Secretary sent a message in 1939 saying that Englishmen were going to fight'. There is a real difficulty here in that the Foreign Secretary would have had to act in an official capacity, and it is not easy to know what that phrase means; but we will ignore this. We may also ignore the difficulty that other things may also have had to happen, and that the message would not have had to be withdrawn, in general that the analysis may not be complete. But even so the analysis will not do, for the Foreign Secretary, or any other man who normally managed these things, might have been ill or otherwise out of action at the relevant date and still England might have declared war. Thus the action of the Foreign Secretary, though it no doubt did occur, was not merely an insufficient condition of England's declaration of war; it was not a necessary one. The point is that one does not need to know what sort of constitution we have in England, what normal mechanism of declaring war, and what people were well and what were sick in order to understand the statement 'England declared war in 1939'. There is an indefinite range of things that people might have done, any set of which would have counted as England declaring war. There might have been a revolution in 1938 and the war might have been declared by a mass meeting or a revolutionary junta; and this would count as England declaring war. This did not happen; but we can understand the statement 'England declared war in 1939' without knowing that it did not happen. But we cannot write out an indefinite range of doings by people, though we can give examples. Therefore we cannot analyse nation statements into statements about people, and therefore we cannot say that England or any other nation is a logical construction out of people. For it is not merely practically impossible to complete the analysis as might have been the case if we had to enumerate everybody's activities; an indefinitely long list of alternative ways of declaring war could not be completed even in theory.

Now the case of nations is a particularly annoying example to have gone wrong, in two ways. First, to say that people or things were logical constructions out of sense-data had always been a bit dashing; some, such as Dr. Johnson, have thought it to be highly paradoxical; one needs a good deal of philosophical conditioning to be able to accept it, and even the best conditioned may have their moments of doubt. If reductive analysis had been found impossible only in these cases then analysts might have said, without suffering the worst pangs, that perhaps physical objects were after all basic objects of acquaintance. We may take it that they would have said this rather than doubt the method of analysis. But the analyst had no doubt that states were not basic objects of acquaintance; and here he felt that he had the man in the street on his side.

One needed philosophical conditioning to believe in states and nations as self-subsistent objects, not to disbelieve in them. Common sense and empiricism combined to convince the analyst on this point; it was preferable to admit that the method of reductive analysis was powerless to deal with the philosophical problems about the nature of the state than to admit that states were basic entities. If the method requires that either statements about states be analysed into equivalent statements about people, or states be admitted among the ultimate constituents of the world, then there is something wrong with the method.

The second particularly annoying thing about this case was that it seemed so clear that we learn the meaning of statements about nations by reference to just such statements about individual men as were offered as analyses of them and that in order to verify such a statement as that England declared war it is of precisely such statements about the actions of individual men that the truth must be ascertained. It was particularly hard to see how in these circumstances there could fail to be identity of meaning. And yet, it seemed, the fact was all too clear: while statements about the actions of Englishmen could be found which provided all the information requisite for us to know that England declared war, while such statements were just what was needed to make clear just what it was for England to declare war, there was no logical equivalence between the alleged analysis and the analysandum. The fault of the analyses did not therefore appear to consist in saying too little—it did not seem that they failed by omitting to refer to some extra entity, for example—if anything, they seemed to provide too detailed an account of what was said in the analysandum. Thus the failure to achieve a satisfactory analysis was especially perplexing, and was not of a kind which led the analysts to accept the view that states were after all basic ingredients in the world.

But though these difficulties about the analysis of statements about nations were particularly annoying, since they were prima facie among the most promising candidates, much more dust was raised in the controversial attempt to give a phenomenalistic analysis of statements about material objects, to show that they were logical constructions out of sense-data. Since we are now concerned primarily to illustrate the general difficulties which beset all attempts to give new-level analyses, we may neglect the controversy as to whether an analysis of a phenomenalistic type was sufficient, or whether some reference to a 'physical occupant' was also necessary; we also need not commit the historical solecism of querying the use of the term 'sense-datum'. These difficulties, however real, are irrelevant to the point with which we are now concerned.

Let us start our inquiry by examining a crude and careless analysis such as Berkeley gave. He first suggests, in effect, that we may analyse 'There is a desk in my room' into 'I have a deskish sense-datum'.[1] But, recognizing that the original might be true when he was out of the room, he suggests that in those circumstances it means that someone (perhaps God) has a deskish sense-datum, or that he himself would have one if he were to go back into the room. Now Berkeley's first suggestion will not do for three reasons:

(i) To say that there is a desk in my room is not to say anything more about my sense-datum than about anyone else's.

(ii) Even if I am in my room and can see my desk, when I say merely that there is a desk in my room I do not say that I am having any sense-data of it. Berkeley's alternative analyses absurdly suggest that one means something different by saying that there is a desk in a room when one can see it from what one means when one cannot. We can thus enlarge on (i) above by saying that to say that there is a desk in my room is to say nothing about what I or anybody else can now

---

[1] *Principles of Human Knowledge*, para. 3.

see. (Even if God can see the desk all the time, we do not say so.)

(iii) I might have a deskish sense-datum when in my room and yet there be no desk there; I might have an hallucination or be tricked by mirrors, &c. Therefore in addition to the rider on (ii) that there being a desk in my room does not entail my seeing it, or anyone else seeing it, we have conversely the point that my, or anybody else's, deskish sense-datum does not entail the desk being there.

Faced by these difficulties we seem to be thrown back on the hypothetical analysis suggested by Berkeley, though not, of course, in the crude form in which he gave it. This was the conclusion of most of the analysts of the period, which was technically put by saying that the analysis of statements about physical objects which do not include the statement that someone is, or has been, sensibly aware of them must be in terms only of possible and not of actual sense-data. A statement about a physical object must be a statement about what can be seen, felt, &c., under suitable conditions. This is clearly similar to Mill's doctrine that a physical object is a permanent possibility of sensation. But to say so much is not to give an analysis but only to specify that the analysis must be in terms of hypothetical statements about what sense-data people would have in certain circumstances.

There are a number of difficulties in giving an analysis in terms of sense-data which we need only indicate, as foreign to our present interest. For example, there is the difficulty of specifying sense-data except in terms of physical objects; thus we have spoken about deskish sense-data. It was common to ascribe this difficulty to the poverty of our language. Next, there is the difficulty of how we are to frame the protases of our hypothetical statements; is it legitimate to say 'If I were in the room . . . ' when the room is the kind of thing which is being analysed? Some phenomenalists answered that in principle (blessed phrase) they could specify the situation in terms of sense-data, but it was clearly a very complicated matter. But we shall waive all difficulties of this kind since they are not illustrative of the general problem of analysis.

With these concessions made let us suppose we have an analysis of 'There is a desk in the room' beginning: 'If Jones were in the room he would be having deskish sense-data. . . .' Now it is clear that if 'There is a desk in the room' is equivalent to this hypothetical plus others, then if this hypothetical is false the statement that there is a desk in the room will be false also. For, generally, if p is equivalent to the conjunction of q, r, and s, then not-q entails not-p. But it is clear that if Jones comes into the room he may not notice the desk or he may be blind or . . . . Then the hypothetical will be false, and if it is part of the analysis of the physical object statement we shall have to count it also false, which is absurd. Therefore, as it stands, the hypothetical cannot be part of the analysis. Now if there were a definite number of circumstances in which Jones might fail to see the desk this difficulty could be easily circumvented. We should merely complicate the protasis in some such way as 'If Jones were to come into the room and look in the right direction and not be physically blind or psychically blind then . . . '. But there is no definite list of the things which might go wrong; an unspecifiable number of different things might prevent Jones seeing the desk. If we make the protasis strong enough it will be by such a device as saying 'If Jones comes in and sees veridically (or correctly) . . .'; then he certainly will have the sense-data as a matter of logic and the hypothetical will boil down to 'If Jones comes into the room and has the sense-data he will have them', which says nothing. Thus it would seem that the analysis cannot start; there is nothing logically entailed about what anyone will see in certain circumstances by a statement about physical objects, however good grounds it may give for confidence that in fact he will see certain things.

But even if we could see our way round this difficulty and

could allow that the analysis could start, we find that the analysis could not finish. For if the group of sense-datum statements is to be equivalent to the physical object statement then the occurrence of the sense-data must be a necessary and sufficient condition of the truth of the physical object statement. Now many analysts doubted whether any finite set of sense-data could ever be a sufficient condition for the truth of a statement about a physical object; however many hypotheticals had been verified it was logically possible that in the future as many more should be falsified; no statement about a physical object could be conclusively established. But we may refuse to admit this and say that after so many sense-datum statements have been verified the physical object statement becomes certain; we may say that no experience could make us doubt that there is a nose on our face now, even if it were tomorrow to disappear without trace or change into a door-knob.[1] In that way we could perhaps save the view that it was possible to give a finite set of hypotheticals about sense-data which would be a sufficient condition of the truth of a physical object statement. But it is clearly not a necessary condition that those particular sense-datum statements should have been the verified ones; others would have done as well. Thus we cannot get a finite set of hypothetical statements about sense-data which are a necessary condition of the truth of a physical object statement, and perhaps not a set constituting a sufficient condition. But if there is not a precise finite set then the analysis is impossible.

Thus the position may be summarized as follows: (a) any statement about a physical object which does not include the assertion that it is perceived must be analysed, if analysable at all, in terms of the possibility of having sense-data, not of actual sense-data; but (b) there are no circumstances in which the presence of a physical object logically entails that

[1] See Ayer, 'Phenomenalism', *Proceedings of the Aristotelian Society*, 1946.

it will be seen, that sense-data will be obtained, so that one cannot say ever that if there is a physical object in a certain place the possibility of this person having this sense-datum is part of what is meant by saying so; and (c) it is impossible to give a list of possible sense-data the occurrence of which would be sufficient grounds for the assertion of the existence of a physical object and at the same time be a necessary condition of the truth of the assertion—but an analysis must be the necessary and sufficient condition of the analysandum. Point (b) is equivalent to saying that the analysis could never start, point (c) to saying that if it could start it could not finish. It is worth while to add that it is not the phenomenalistic character of the proposed analysis which causes the trouble, since the addition of a clause asserting the existence of a physical occupant or substance would not save the inadequacy of the rest of the analysis.

Once again, the analyst who came face to face with such difficulties as these felt thwarted, for though the view that physical objects were logical constructions out of sense-data had always been recognized as more risky than the view that nations were logical constructions out of people it seemed that no serious inadequacy of his view was revealed by these difficulties; he was being defeated by what seemed much more like technical quibbles. It still seemed to the analyst that only sense-data were required as grounds for the assertion of the existence of a physical object and that a statement about a physical object could lead only to the expectation of sense-data. But no serious analyst who demanded rigour could simply disregard the difficulties, and there seemed to be no way of disposing of all of them.

The reader, indeed, may not find these arguments against the possibility of analysis as conclusive as they seemed at the time and as they have therefore been presented here. If we revert temporarily to the simpler case of the analysis of statements about nations we may put the case as follows. At the level of talk about nations, it may be said, such a statement as that England declared war is a very indefinite and imprecise statement; having been told this we might still ask what exactly England did. The failure to analyse therefore arose from the insistence that the analysandum should be equivalent to some quite definite statement about what individuals did. But it might still be possible to find an equivalence between such statements about nations and equally indefinite and imprecise statements about what individual men did. Every objection to proposed analyses took the form of denying that what the analysis said was precisely what the analysandum said, which was true only because the analysandum did not say anything precisely.

We need not now weigh carefully the merits of this contention, though it clearly contains a great deal of truth. The important thing to see is that to make such a defence of analytic procedures involves the abandonment of the whole attitude to language accepted by both the earlier atomists and the logical positivists. Language had been conceived as a clearcut truth-functional structure, securely based on atomic propositions; given this view of language indefinite statements, though their occurrence could not be ignored completely, had seemed to be aberrations presenting a very special problem. Such a view of language had seemed essential to empiricism, since it showed how the edifice of our knowledge was securely based on experience; to give it up involved as radical a change of view as the abandonment of the view that all our conceptual apparatus was built up out of simple ideas would have meant for Locke. Such a defence of analysis as we have suggested was therefore impossible for the analysts since in employing it they would have abandoned their whole conception of the purpose and nature of analysis.

So the analysis which for both the logical atomist and the logical positivist had been the central activity of philosophers was seen, after and as a result of the most patient efforts, to be impossible of achievement except in comparatively trivial cases, outside the field of mathematical logic in which Russell had scored his successes. The view of philosophy as having its task in the reductive analysis of the puzzling statements of our ordinary everyday language to the simple atomic reports of immediate experience had to be abandoned. This could not be the way to reveal either the structure of the world or the structure of our language.

Though it would be absurd to suggest that all analysts saw this point clearly and immediately—one does not see clearly in a crisis—we can none the less easily observe in the literature of the late thirties a growing recognition that reductive analysis must at least reduce its claims. As it was out of the question for empiricists to admit that statements about nations, things, and people, and everything except the llama and the average plumber, were all basic, nor did the difficulties in reductive analysis point to such a conclusion, some other solution had to be found. There were two obvious alternatives. Faced with the difficulties about the thesis that language was truth-functional which we noticed earlier and now with the difficulties in reductive analysis, philosophers could not go on maintaining seriously that ordinary language was even a very inexplicit and untidy version of a truth-functional calculus provided with a vocabulary; nor was it possible to regard it as an inexplicit version of any other calculus.

One alternative was therefore to say 'so much the worse for ordinary languages'. In so far as ordinary, natural languages are not, in principle, either truth-functional or modelled on some other calculus they are faulty, unsuitable as objects of scientific philosophical investigation, vague muddles best forgotten in the study. Reductive analysis is impossible in natural languages because they are too amorphous and indefinite; we must construct more and better artificial languages to study and, so far as possible, to use in their place. This is, in principle, the line taken by Carnap and his associates. If the statements made by these philosophers about language seem so often grotesquely wrong to those accustomed to the English philosophical climate, it must be remembered that they are not talking about the natural languages that we are interested in. The corresponding misunderstanding on their side is their tendency to think that our interest in natural languages shows us to be an odd kind of social scientist interested in the natural history of language and barely philosophers at all. There is at present a failure to communicate. But as this alternative was chosen by few philosophers in England we cannot now pursue its merits and demerits.

The other alternative is to stick to ordinary language as our tool and object of study, in so far as we study language. The obvious, simple reason for choosing this alternative is that it is such statements as that there is a table here, that Jones is thinking, that England is democratic, and that we ought to love our neighbour that puzzle us philosophically and require our examination rather than some other less septic utterances which may or may not be of interest. We want to know what it is that we call 'knowledge' in our everyday thought, not what we might have talked about instead by uttering that noise in a new and improved language. But if we accept this alternative we have as a consequence to abandon the truth-functional view of language and therewith the view that language consists of a vast array of completely simple reports of experience, of which the statements of ordinary English, German, and French are abbreviated conjunctions and disjunctions; the ancient doctrine of British empiricism that all non-simple concepts are complexes of simple concepts must finally go. We have not merely to think of a new justification of traditional analysis, we have to get a new conception of philosophy which we may or may not call analysis. This was the alternative which, in one way or another, most English philosophers chose.

This way of putting things must not be accepted too literally. There was not a moment when this decision suddenly presented itself clear-cut to philosophers. Philosophers did not accept the second alternative and then start their search for a new way of doing philosophy. No doubt the difficulties in analysis slowly dawned on them, and they made *ad hoc* retreats and modifications as the various points occurred to them one after another; they were able to embrace the second alternative because they already found a different conception and method of philosophizing forcing itself upon them. The analysts, then, did not consciously face the problems in the order that we have set them out, one by one; at the most we can hope to have presented a fair rationalization of the situation.

Here, then, our account of the rise and fall of reductive analysis in England between the two great wars comes to an end. It remains to give some indication of the new conception of philosophy which began to emerge from the ruins of the old.

PART III

THE BEGINNINGS OF CONTEMPORARY PHILOSOPHY

11

THE BEGINNINGS OF CONTEMPORARY PHILOSOPHY

THIS part of our discussion must begin with some explanations of its scope and aims. First a few words must be said about the scope of the expression 'contemporary philosophy' in the title. No world-survey of the contemporary scene, nor even a comprehensive survey of the origins of all philosophical trends in England today, is intended. The contemporary philosophy with the origins of which we are concerned is that of which Wittgenstein and Wisdom in Cambridge, Ryle, Waismann, and Austin in Oxford, may be mentioned as prominent exponents; at the time of writing most of the younger philosophers in Oxford hold the sort of views with which we shall be concerned. But though this way of philosophizing had its origins largely in Cambridge and, numerically, is most strongly represented now in Oxford, there are many who think in similar ways not merely in other English universities, but in other continents.

Now it is not possible to write a history of a set of philosophical investigations which are still in progress; that is one quite decisive reason against any attempt to give a comprehensive account of the work of these philosophers. Further, these philosophers do not constitute a school or movement. No doubt the division of philosophers into schools is always a somewhat artificial matter, since every philosopher worthy of the name will say what he thinks whether it agrees with the thoughts of his colleagues or no; but it was not too arbitrary to refer to the logical positivist movement, for a number of philosophers did accept this name for their philosophy, even when they preferred some variant on it (e.g. logical empiricism), and held in common as basic tenets the view of philosophy as analysis of language, the rejection of metaphysics, and the verification theory of meaning. The contemporary philosophers we are now considering, however, do not accept any common title; such as are given them are applied dyslogistically by their opponents (e.g. therapeutic positivism). This unwillingness to accept a common title reflects an absence of shared basic tenets; most of these philosophers fight shy of the sort of general philosophical pronouncements which could count as basic tenets. In any case, apart from a reluctance to subscribe in common to any general formula, there is a good deal of quite serious disagreement amongst them; while there is undoubtedly a 'family resemblance' between their views and their methods it would be hard to find a description, however loose and elastic, which would apply to all or even most.

These facts make it impossible to attempt a general account of even a circumscribed portion of the contemporary scene, whatever the historian of the future may find himself in a position to say. But there is a less ambitious programme which does seem possible of achievement. In the late thirties a few articles appeared written in a way very different from that of classical analysis and much more akin to the work of philosophers of the present day. Moreover, these articles, together with the oral arguments of their authors, undoubtedly had a powerful influence upon the contemporary philosophers with whom we are concerned. We may reasonably hope by a discussion of these articles to throw some light on the genesis of the views and methods of these philosophers. That will be our limited aim.

A. THE PURPOSE OF ANALYSIS

Even at the beginning of the thirties Ryle had written an article with the title 'Systematically Misleading Expressions'.[1] In this article he considered a number of types of expression which he considered to be systematically misleading—Quasi-ontological Statements (Mr. Baldwin is objective, Mr. Pickwick subjective), Quasi-Platonic Statements (colour involves extension), Quasi-descriptions, &c. He then asked what he had been doing in his examination of these expressions and concludes:

I conclude that there is after all a sense in which we can properly enquire and even say 'what it really means to say so and so'. For we can ask what is the real form of the fact recorded when this is concealed or disguised and not duly exhibited by the expression in question. And we can often succeed in stating this fact in a new form of words which does exhibit what the other failed to exhibit. And I am for the present inclined to believe that this is what philosophical analysis is, and that this is the sole and whole function of philosophy. . . . But as confession is good for the soul, I must admit that I do not very much relish the conclusions to which these conclusions point. I would rather allot to philosophy a sublimer task than the detection of the sources in linguistic idioms of recurrent misconstructions and absurd theories. But that it is at least this I cannot feel serious doubt.

This is an interesting quotation; in parts it reads like the old analytic doctrine of the logical atomists—the philosopher is engaged in restating propositions which do not exhibit the real form of the fact in a way in which the form will be duly exhibited. But a new point of this analysis is suggested; our aim is no longer the ontological one of getting

[1] *Proceedings of the Aristotelian Society*, 1931–2; reprinted in *Logic and Language*, vol. i, ed. Flew.

a clearer view of the structure of reality but to clear up puzzlement, prevent misconstruction of language, and expose absurd theories. Thus 'Mr. Baldwin is a politician' does exhibit the form of the fact, is not in need of analysis, and is hence not misleading; 'Mr. Baldwin is objective' does not exhibit the form of the fact, does need analysis, and without analysis is misleading. Still the obscure reference to the form of the fact is there, but, like the human appendix, it seems vestigial and without a function. It seems that Ryle could have skipped a stage and simply said that 'Mr. Baldwin is a politician' is an expression which does not mislead us and hence needs no philosophical treatment, whereas 'Mr. Baldwin is objective' is an expression which does mislead into absurd theories and inferences, so that the philosopher has the task of putting what it says into another verbal form which does not mislead us in this way. Ryle did not see this at the time, nor did anyone else.

Things were however soon to be taken still further. In 1937 Ayer was to say.[1]

We are faced with the problem of determining what it is that gives an analysis, or a definition, a philosophical character. . . . I suggest that the answer should refer not to the form of the analysis, but rather to the effect of it on us. The common sense propositions which call for philosophical analysis are those which are formulated in such a way that they encourage us to draw false inferences, or ask spurious questions, or make nonsensical assumptions. Thus, propositions about nations call for philosophical analysis because they lead us to treat nations as if they were magnified persons, and propositions about material things call for it because they encourage belief in a physical world 'behind' the world of phenomena, and propositions containing definite descriptive phrases call for it because they give rise to the postulation of subsistent entities, and existential propositions call for it because

[1] 'Does Philosophy Analyse Common Sense?' *Proceedings of the Aristotelian Society*, supplementary volume xvi, p. 173.

of the ontological argument. And philosophy in one way or another tries to remove all these dangers.

I say 'in one form or another' because I do not think that all processes of philosophical analysis are of a single form. . . . That is to say, I should not now maintain that the activity of philosophizing consisted solely in the provision of translations.

The relation of this quotation to that from Ryle is quite clear. The need for philosophical treatment of an expression is now directly connected to its misleading character without reference to the form of facts, and it is consequently realized that the treatment need not be in the form of a translation. Other techniques may be used; the criterion of adequacy is the success in showing up what is misleading in the expression. But in both Ryle and Ayer the aim is clearly stated to be the avoidance of being misled by language. No longer is the aim the discovery of the logical concatenation of facts or the structure of a language; for those aims language has to be calculus-like; for the new aim it has not.

B. THE NATURE OF METAPHYSICS

Ryle had suggested that one thing which made the statement 'Mr. Baldwin is objective' misleading was that its superficial grammatical similarity to 'Mr. Baldwin is a politician' might lead us to think that the two expressions were similar in their whole logical character. This suggestion can be generalized. It might be suggested that the superficial grammatical similarity of all sentences in the indicative mood might lead to expectations of some general similarity in their logical character, in spite of specific differences; for, after all, it was only with great difficulty and a sense of considerable achievement that philosophers had come to recognize the important distinction between synthetic and analytic propositions. In particular, it might be suggested that, in offering the verification principle as a single criterion of meaning for all indicative sentences save analytic ones, the logical positivists had been led by superficial grammatical resemblance into thinking that any expression having the same grammar as the empirical statements with regard to which the verification principle seemed most plausible must either have the same logical character as they had or else be faulty, nonsensical.

Certainly the verification principle was giving trouble in the late thirties. Philosophers did not merely find trouble in determining its exact formulation; there were more serious difficulties. According to the logical positivists any scientific use of language must be the utterance either of a tautology or of an empirical statement; that, combined with a view about the nature of empirical statements, was what the verification principle in effect said. But what then is the status of the verification principle itself? That is the awkward question which had to be considered. Clearly the holder of the principle must say that it is a tautology, a rule of language, or that it is an empirical proposition. Some early critics of positivism had thought that the positivists would say that it was an empirical proposition. But this is absurd. First, it was a philosophers' statement, and no philosophers' statement can be empirical according to the positivist. Philosophy is for him tautological clarification of language. Secondly, it was quite clear that positivists did not put forward the principle as a generalization resulting from an exhaustive study of metaphysical statements, all of which had been found meaningless independently of the principle. Nor were they prepared to examine all metaphysical statements on their merits and perhaps one day admit that this or that metaphysical statement is an exception and is meaningful; at the most one produced a few examples of peculiar metaphysical utterances as examples, and perhaps diagnosed what sort of linguistic confusion they embodied. Thirdly, it was quite clear that those who proposed the verification principle were trying to show that, independently of detailed examination, it could be seen that a metaphysical statement *must* be meaningless. It is evident then, as Ayer for example claimed, that the verification principle had to be called *a priori* by its supporters. But this alternative was by no means a happy one, since for the positivist all *a priori* propositions are rules of language of a conventional character. If the positivist admits that the verification principle is an arbitrary rule for the use of the word 'meaningful', then his opponent has only to say that he is not going to follow this new-fangled way of speaking; he will go on using the old sense of 'meaningful', whatever its definition may be, according to which metaphysics is meaningful. If, on the other hand, the verificationist takes the line that the verification principle is a rule of language for the use of the word 'meaningful' which is implicit in ordinary discourse, it is a hard saying. It would not be a paradox to say that some statements of some sorts had always been meaningless, according to the conventional sense of 'meaningless', but people had just not detected that they were meaningless; this might be true of, say, some statements about absolute motion. But the positivist was rejecting whole classes of statements which had always been accepted as meaningful. All ethics and theology went by the board, for example. It is hard to swallow the doctrine that one has always used the concept of 'sense' in such a way that 'this is good' is nonsense—harder to swallow than a good deal of theology. Whether the verification principle was in accord with ordinary usage seems then to be an empirical question easily decided in the negative. It was hard then to maintain that the verification principle was either empirical or a tautology.

In his 'Metaphysics and Verification'[1] Wisdom wrote:

Well, shall we accept the verification principle? What is it to accept it? When people bring out with a dashing air the words 'The meaning of a statement is really simply the method of its verification', like one who says 'The value of a thing is really simply its power of exchange', in what sort of way are they using

[1] *Mind*, 1938, p. 454.

words? What is the general nature of their theory? The answer is 'It is a metaphysical theory'.

So the verification principle is neither empirical, nor tautological, but metaphysical! Of course, opponents had said before that the verification principle was metaphysical, but that had seemed mere malice. It was a much more serious matter coming from Wisdom. But what does it mean to call it metaphysical? Some light will be thrown on this by an examination of a passage in C. L. Stevenson's 'Persuasive Definitions' in which he writes:[1]

Let us now proceed to a more recent issue. Positivism achieved its wide appeal before Carnap's 'principle of tolerance', and achieved it largely through the statement, 'Metaphysics is without meaning'. But isn't this remark surprisingly like that of the nineteenth-century critics, who said that Pope was 'not a poet'? The Positivists were stating an unquestionable fact in their sense of meaning, just as the nineteenth-century critics were, in their sense of poet. The truth of such statements, however, is utterly beside the point. Controversy hinges on the emotive words that are used. Shall we define 'meaning' narrowly, so that science alone will receive this laudatory title, and metaphysics the correspondingly derogatory one of 'nonsense'? Shall our terminology show science in a fine light, and metaphysics in a poor one? Shall we, in short, accept this *persuasive* definition of 'meaning'? This is the question, though well concealed by the dictum that definitions are 'merely arbitrary'.

But this conclusion deserves careful qualification. We must remember that the nineteenth-century critics, to return to the analogy, were not condemning Pope with sheer bombast. They were also making a distinction. Their narrow sense of 'poet' had the function of stressing, to the reader's attention, certain features common to most poetry, but lacking in Pope's. Perhaps they meant to say this: 'We have long been blind to fundamental differences between Pope's work and that of a Shakespeare or Milton. It is because of this blindness alone that we have been content to give Pope a laudatory title. Let us note the difference, then, and deprive him

[1] *Mind*, 1938, pp. 339–40.

of his title.' The contention of the Positivists will easily bear the same interpretation. Perhaps they meant to say: 'We have long been blind to the fundamental differences between the use of sentences in science and their use in metaphysics. It is because of this blindness alone that we have been content to dignify metaphysics with such titles as "meaningful". Let us define meaning, then, in a way that will at once stress these fundamental differences, and deprive metaphysics of its title.' When thus stated the positivistic thesis has not only heat but light, and is not to be scorned. And yet, perhaps there is still too much heat for the amount of light. It is of no little service to stress the ways in which metaphysics has been confused with science; and to the extent that positivists have done this, their 'conquest of metaphysics' has not depended on exhortation. But do their distinctions take us more than *half way* to a full rejection of metaphysics? Are we led to go the other half by the word 'nonsense', defined so that it may cast its objectionable emotive meaning upon metaphysics, without being predicated of it untruthfully?

The same question arises even when metaphysics is denied cognitive meaning only. 'Cognitive' is used to mean 'empirically verifiable or else analytic', and with exclusive laudatory import. Hence the positivistic contention reduces to this: 'Metaphysical statements are neither empirically verifiable nor analytic; hence they are not respectable.' If metaphysicians answer, 'Our statements, even though neither empirically verifiable nor analytic, are still respectable', they are scarcely to be led away from their position by mere exhortation.

Stevenson goes on to say that what is really required is a careful examination of the actual nature both of science and of metaphysics and less emotional heat.

Thus we find Wisdom calling the verification principle a piece of metaphysics and Stevenson calling it a demand to distinguish more radically between metaphysics and science, combined with an expression of preference for science. It must on no account be thought that Wisdom and Stevenson are disagreeing here. Wisdom, in this new phase, would have agreed with what Stevenson said, if not, perhaps, to the exact formulation, and would have added that this is typical of the sort of thing which metaphysicians are always doing. Metaphysicians may be muddled and may consistently use misleading language, but it is no use simply to dismiss what they say as nonsense; one must patiently examine what they are doing, and perhaps it will not always be wholly bad. The verification principle may be muddled and be bad in so far as it suggests that we should not examine what metaphysicians do; but it also, in however warped a manner, draws attention to the fundamental difference between science and metaphysics.

The last few paragraphs have had the continuation of the history of the verification principle only as a subordinate purpose. Much more important is the fact that Wisdom and Stevenson are no longer willing to say that the principle is a tautology, or that it is metaphysical, merely as a piece of abuse. Nor do they merely say that it is metaphysical as though that is something which we all immediately understand; they attempt to indicate clearly what sort of a point it has. In doing this Stevenson invokes a use of language not previously recognized, a use of indicative sentences to which the simple dichotomies, analytic–synthetic, true–false, tautological–self-contradictory are not applicable. The recognition of this richer variety of uses of language is one of the marks of the new period. The tendency now will be, though not always perfectly realized, to ask questions like 'What are people doing when they use ethical, scientific, metaphysical language, claim knowledge, or express belief, make promises, or express sympathy?' without trying to fit them all into a few *a priori* categories.

We have considered in detail Stevenson's account of the verification principle. But an article by Wisdom had already appeared in which he had attempted to give a general account of the puzzling and paradoxical questions and answers to which philosophers have been addicted, of which the verification principle is but one example. Since this article was the

first which throughout embodied the new philosophical outlook, it is something of a landmark in the history of philosophy;
we need offer no excuses for treating it in some detail. To
those who are acquainted with later developments it may now
seem somewhat tame, a little oversimplified, and quite easy
to follow. But when it was first published it was a decided
novelty, so much so as to be intelligible only with the greatest
difficulty to those who were not primed by the oral discussions in Cambridge at that time.

The first significant thing about the article is its title,
'Philosophical Perplexity'.[1] It had always been assumed that
the job of philosophers was to answer questions, to solve
problems, even if all the problems were limited to the analytic
questions 'Is p equivalent to q?', 'Can sentences which contain the expression X be replaced by equivalent sentences
containing instead the expression Y?'. What philosophers said
would be true or false, even if only in the sense in which
tautologies are true and contradictions false. But this title
suggests that philosophers are not propounding solutions to
problems, answering questions, putting forward theories, but
are rather grappling with puzzlement, trying to put themselves straight where they are confused; to do philosophy is
less like trying to discover some elusive facts than trying to
find one's way out of a maze. A favourite way of putting this
point was to say that philosophical problems needed not to
be solved but to be dissolved. All this cannot, of course, be
grasped from the title alone, but it is reasonable to suppose
that such considerations were in the author's mind when he
chose the title.

Wisdom starts by saying that philosophical questions are
really requests for a ruling on the use of sentences in matters
where there is no clear-cut answer to be derived from
ordinary usage, and that philosophical statements are really

---

[1] *Proceedings of the Aristotelian Society*, vol. xvi, 1936. Reprinted in
Philosophy and Psycho-Analysis.

verbal recommendations made in respose to such requests. The similarity of this to Stevenson's account of the verification principle as a persuasive definition will be immediately seen. Wisdom does not, of course, mean that they are usually intended to be such, but that this is a way of interpreting them which brings out their genuine point. But, he immediately adds, the point of making these statements is not merely to make a verbal recommendation, but to do something else— to clarify, to get a better understanding of the language which we in fact use. Wisdom gives examples to show the kind of thing that he has in mind, but instead of these we shall consider another which would probably have been equally acceptable to Wisdom, an example with a direct bearing on the controversies of the logical atomists which we have already examined. If Wisdom's views are correct we shall thus succeed in simultaneously illustrating them and further clarifying those older controversies. When examining the difficulties presented to logical atomism by general propositions we had occasion to consider Ramsey's later views about general propositions in which he recanted his former view that they could be regarded as infinite conjunctions, the view that 'All A is B' could be regarded as equivalent to 'This A is B, that A is B . . . .', and finally concluded 'If it (the general proposition) is not a conjunction it is not a proposition at all'. Applying Wisdom's arguments in 'Philosophical Perplexity' to this view of Ramsey's we may construe Wisdom as denying that in saying that a so-called general proposition is not a proposition at all Ramsey is reporting a discovery that people have always made a factual error in thinking that so-called general propositions were propositions, like the factual error that many people have made in taking the whale to be a fish. Rather, Wisdom claims, Ramsey is to be regarded as making a verbal recommendation that we should no longer call general propositions propositions, but call them something else, Ramsey's own suggestion being that we should call them rules for framing singular judgements. But, if this is what Ramsey is doing, how does he differ from a philologist who, say, recommends that we should not call television 'radio' but 'video'? Not, Wisdom answers, in what he is doing but in the point of what he is doing. The point of the philologist's recommendation is to get people to talk differently; the point of Ramsey's recommendation is to get people to see how utterly different is that logic of general propositions from the logic of singular propositions; for if we continue to use the word 'proposition' of two so different types of thing there is a danger, into which many philosophers have in fact fallen, of our thinking that they have very much more in common, and differ far less, than Ramsey will admit is the case. In his paper Ramsey very properly tries to list the important dissimilarities which he thinks philosophers have tended to overlook. The justification of Ramsey's recommendations, if they are justifiable at all and not merely ill-advised, is that if we accept them we shall not fall into philosophical perplexity in the way that we did before; a philosophical gain is made, there is no question of it being a mere matter of convenience. We shall no longer be puzzled about how propositions can be either singular or general.

To quote Wisdom directly: 'Philosophical theories are illuminating . . . when they suggest or draw attention to a terminology which reveals likenesses and differences which are concealed by ordinary language.' It will be noted that Wisdom says 'concealed' and is not content to say that these likenesses and differences are merely not made explicit. Now inasmuch as the disguised and misconceived way in which philosophers' recommendations have been made, usually in the guise of factual statements, has concealed from people their true nature and has led us to be perplexed about the nature of philosophy, they are themselves examples of confusion. But, Wisdom says, 'philosophical theories exhibit both linguistic confusion and linguistic penetration', and he considers that in the recent past too much attention has been given to the element of confusion in philosophical theories, with the result, for example, that they have been called meaningless by the positivists. Though there has, no doubt, been bad philosophy in the past, the element of confusion should not blind us to the value of much classical philosophy.

Another point emphasized by Wisdom is that in making their disguised recommendations philosophers tend to concentrate on one set of similarities and differences at the expense of others. Wisdom tries to make this clear, and at the same time develop his thesis, by using as an illustration his own philosophical statement that philosophers' statements are really verbal recommendations; this, being a philosophical statement, is itself a disguised verbal recommendation. The question is how to place philosophical statements with respect both to philologists' statements about language and also to ordinary statements in which words are used but which are not about them, and by saying that philosophers' statements are really verbal Wisdom is apparently recommending that they should be classified with philologists' statements. But this involves us in neglect of the purpose of philosophical statements; it brings out the likeness between the statement of the philologist: ' "Monarchy" means "a set of people under a king" ' and the statement of the philosopher: 'A monarchy is a set of people under a king', but it fails to bring out the difference which, following Wisdom, we have called a difference of point. Wisdom tries to bring this out by heading the first section of his paper 'Philosophical statements are really verbal' and the second 'Philosophical statements are not verbal', bringing out in the appropriate section the two sets of likenesses and differences. It is best in the end, not to say that philosophical statements are verbal or factual, for both are misleading; they are philosophical statements. To bring out what inclines one to call them verbal and what equally rightly inclines one to deny it is, however, a good way to make people clearer about philosophy. One will then no longer be perplexed and hampered by these competing inclinations. Clearly the bare statement that philosophical statements are neither statements of fact nor verbal will merely suppress our puzzlement, not cure it. The desire to make recommendations one way or the other is itself a sign of philosophical perplexity. It would be idle, and unhelpful, to ban them; but if one comes to see them for what they are one will regard them in a different light, as emphatic expository devices which can be dispensed with and are not to be taken at their face value.

We earlier attempted to illustrate Wisdom's paper by an examination of Ramsey's view of general propositions; in fact the main part of this paper is devoted to working out in considerable detail another example of how the thesis can be applied. I shall summarize this example. Wisdom takes the case of those who say, with an air of disillusioned factual discovery, that we can never really know anything beyond the sphere of mathematics and our immediate experience. This air of factual discovery is misleading, Wisdom claims, because (1) those who make such statements have not found something unreliable about the things that we ordinarily say we know; (2) they do not in fact exhibit any signs of practical doubt on these matters; (3) if we took them seriously and started saying, in all spheres outside mathematics and immediate experience, 'probably' and 'perhaps' the effect these words have of enjoining caution would quickly be lost. They have an effect precisely because we do not use them in such an indiscriminate manner. But in spite of these points, Wisdom holds, it is not satisfactory to say that these philosophers are being absurd and metaphysical in the pejorative sense of that word which the positivists employed; they are not merely misusing language. Further, if we baldly say to them 'You are making a verbal recommendation that we should no longer ever say that we know in these contexts and we do

not propose to accept your recommendation', these philosophers will rightly suspect that we have not properly understood them. For these philosophers are making a genuine
point. There is a difference between the cases of mathematical
knowledge and knowledge of immediate experience on the
one hand, and our knowledge of empirical fact on the other.
Types of error are logically possible in the case of empirical
knowledge which are not logically possible in the case of the
two other types of knowledge. For example, it always makes
sense in the case of empirical knowledge 'But perhaps facts
will turn up which will make us abandon this', but this is not
so in the other cases. Thus the difference is genuine and it is
important to recognize it. The mistake of philosophers who
hold the view under discussion is that they fail to see that
there is another distinction, between what we have some
positive ground for feeling practical doubt about and what
leaves no room for serious doubt, and that this is the distinction which is at present marked by the use of 'know' on the
one hand, and 'probably' on the other; consequently in spite
of their insight they are confusing things by proposing to
signalize a logical possibility of error by the language of
probability which is designed to bring out the genuine possibility of error, thus making us feel uncomfortably that we
ought to have serious doubts about the possibility of induc-
tive knowledge, knowledge based on memory, and the like.
The only right thing to do, here as elsewhere, is both to show
the point of the philosophical assertion and also to bring out
its misleading character.

Such, in barest outline, are the contents of Wisdom's
paper, which all should read. Though probably neither Wisdom nor anyone else would now put things in precisely this
way it is none the less the first manifesto of a new way of doing
philosophy. In philosophical method it is far more similar to
present-day work than to anything which had preceded it.[1]

[1] In a footnote Wisdom expressed a great debt to Wittgenstein, while

C. TWO NEW SLOGANS

In the light of this summary exposition of the new doctrines we can try to understand two precepts which gained currency at this period. In place of the dogmatic 'The meaning of a statement is the method of its verification' we were now advised 'Don't ask for the meaning, ask for the use' and told that 'Every statement has its own logic'. These are, of course, only slogans, and were so called by those who used them, but it is worth while to investigate them. The slogan 'Don't ask for the meaning, ask for the use' warns us to stop asking 'What is the analysis (the meaning) of this statement?', expecting to find some equivalent statement, complying probably with some preconceived requirements, and being dissatisfied if we fail; instead we are to ask what is done by the use of the statement. If, for example, it is unverifiable, then its job is clearly not to describe the world about us, but perhaps it is used for some quite different purpose. We shall find out by finding out what the utterance of that sentence enables us to do. This task may not be easy, but it is the task of the philosopher. By saying that every statement has its own logic we are giving warning, in language which may perhaps be exaggerated, that we must not expect to find a single task, or even two or three neatly tabulated tasks, which all sentences perform. The logical atomist, for example, had thought that all non-tautological sentences had the single job of describing sense-experience: analysis was necessary to show that those did so which apparently did not.[1] We are now

warning the reader that he was not merely imitating him. It is certain that Wittgenstein had an enormous influence upon, was indeed the main originator of, the new philosophical methods. But as knowledge of his work was at this period limited to a small circle in Cambridge which attended his lectures, it is not possible for us to discuss his contribution. The curious will find in his posthumously published *Philosophical Investigations* material some of which dates back to this period, though it was subsequently revised.

[1] Wittgenstein, in his *Philosophical Investigations*, after listing a score of different uses of language, says: 'It is interesting to compare the

saying that perhaps some statements have a quite different task, and that in any case those statements whose job is in many respects very similar to that of those which report experience may none the less be different in their logic to a degree that prevents us from finding an exact equivalence between them. It is no use trying to patch things up by simply recognizing the one new dimension of 'emotive significance' as some philosophers did at this time. Language has many tasks and many levels; we may or may not be trying to describe the world, and when we do we may do it in radically different ways not reducible to each other. We must on each occasion find what language is being used for without preconceived ideas, especially without the preconception that logically different types of statement will be reducible to one another, and that one type is specially proper or basic. Consequently our approach to philosophical problems will be an attempt to solve each as it arises by what methods we can, rather than to approach them with some preconceived programme.

D. REASSESSMENT OF REDUCTIVE ANALYSIS

In the light of such an attitude we may well ask whether the old reductive analysis with its solitary ideal of translation into basic reports of experience was just a mistake.[1] This is not the line that was taken; indeed it is foreign to the new way of doing philosophy to regard any other way as just a mistake. But the old analysis was regarded with especial sympathy. It is clear, for example, that one way of finding out what job a sentence does is to find another sentence equivalent to it about whose job we are not perplexed and to say 'It does the

multiplicity of the tools in language and of the way they are used, the multiplicity of kinds of word and sentence, with what logicians have said about the structure of language. (Including the author of the *Tractatus Logico-Philosophicus*)', p. 12ᵉ.

[1] This discussion is based principally on Wisdom's 'Metaphysics and Verification', *Mind*, 1938, reprinted in *Philosophy and Psycho-Analysis*.

same job as this one', even if this way is not always open to us. One mistake of the traditional analysts was to think that this method was the only proper method; another was to think that there was some absolute propriety about the one formulation and some impropriety in the other, and to invent a metaphysical explanation of this absolute propriety and impropriety; but the method itself is not faulty. Indeed, even when the method of translation is impossible the old attempts to provide a translation were not wholly misguided. Those who made them were confused in that they failed to see the logical gulf between the analysandum and the alleged analysis; but they were nevertheless doing something worth while. For example, it may be that the language which we use in talking about states is not translatable into the language which we use in talking about individual people, and that translations cannot therefore be successfully made. But the attempts to provide them enable us to see that we can make people understand statements about states by producing more or less equivalent statements about individuals, and that we verify statements about states by the same empirical investigations as we verify these statements about individuals; when we know enough about the behaviour of people we know also the history of states; the history of states is not another branch of history with a different subject-matter alongside the history of individuals. Thus, given the account of the nature of philosophy which requires analysis to be in the form of the provision of equivalences, the attempts of the analysts to deal philosophically with the concept of the state were a series of failures. But if we treat the intended reductive analyses as attempts to show the job that nation-statements do, and if we diagnose rightly the reasons why we have not got complete equivalences, what is otherwise a series of failures can be seen to be of value. Similarly, it is worth while both to compare and to contrast general statements like 'All A is B' with conjunctions of singular propositions.

Perhaps indeed the reason why we cannot find reductive analyses in the case of nation statements is much the same as the reason why the attempts to show that general propositions were equivalent to conjunctions and disjunctions of singular propositions were failures; we are perhaps in both cases using language in logically different ways to achieve much the same purpose.

Thus the attempt to provide equivalences is worth while, providing that at the same time we see why we fail and make it clear that we do fail when we fail. In these circumstances a failure to translate is capable of being a philosophical success. If we see, for example, that our failure to translate statements about nations into statements about people is due to the fact that the point of such a statement as 'England declared war' is precisely to let us know the sort of thing that Englishmen did without saying precisely how, then the failure is unimportant and we are on the way to understanding statements about nations. The analysts had elevated one expedient of philosophical clarification into the very essence of philosophy. Any failure of the expedient was therefore regarded as being the failure to achieve philosophical success instead of being part of one possible way to achieve philosophical success.

In addition to this reassessment of the point of traditional analysis, Wisdom made another point in the same article which is relevant here. Those who spoke of reductive, or new-level, analysis spoke as though by a successful analysis the philosopher was eliminating what he analysed; nations were reduced to individual men, with numbers and chimeras they disappeared from the basic furniture of the world. But this metaphysical goal could never be attained. If Russell analyses 'Two men were there' into 'A man was there and another man was there' then, if we think that we have here a metaphysical elimination of number, we are open to the objection that the notion 'other than' contains already the notion of plurality, of number. If all we want to do is to get clear about the way numbers are used, then no doubt Russell's analysis is very useful; it will, for example, prevent us thinking of them as groups of invisible units. But we cannot turn the numerical into the non-numerical in any way that goes beyond the elimination of the number-words; how otherwise could there be an equivalence? Yet reductive analysis seemed sometimes to be making this mistaken claim. The point can be put in another way as follows: it is not that reductive analysis was successful in some few cases and not in others, so much as that there is no such thing as reductive analysis. Russell's success in analysing numbers did not show that there were really no numbers, and the failure to analyse nations into people did not show that there were nations as well as people in a metaphysically significant sense. Nothing can be reduced to anything else by philosophers, and hence there can be no philosophical successes or failures in this field.

Philosophical method can be taught as well, or better, by example as by precept. Wisdom's point about the mistaken claims of reductive analysis and his claim that philosophers' statements do not report discoveries of fact can be illustrated by reference to another article, by G. A. Paul, entitled 'Is there a Problem about Sense-data?'[1] This article was one of the pre-war articles which were to influence later developments most strongly.

Such philosophers as Moore[2] and Price[3] had argued for the existence, and explained the nature, of sense-data in some such way as follows: when I look at my hand or a tomato I can doubt whether there is anything of the colour I now see, for the light may be bad; I can even wonder whether I am having

---

[1] *Proceedings of the Aristotelian Society*, supplementary volume xv; reprinted in *Logic and Language*, vol. i, ed. Flew.

[2] See, for example, his 'Defence of Common Sense' in *Contemporary British Philosophy*, ed. Muirhead.

[3] *Perception*, ch. i.

a total hallucination and there is perhaps no tomato there at all. But though I can doubt whether there is a physical object having the colour and shape that I see, I cannot doubt that I see *something*; I have some visual experience. This that I cannot have any doubt about is to be called a sense-datum; the existence of sense-data is absolutely certain, and in the nature of the case I can never be deceived about them. The problem of perception was then viewed as being the problem of how physical objects were related to sense-data. Some philosophers were willing to say that on some favourable occasions a sense-datum might be identical with part of the surface of an object; the extreme empiricist line was that tomatoes, hands, and all physical objects were logical constructions out of sense-data, the doctrine known as phenomenalism. It was certain that there were sense-data; the only question was whether physical objects had to be admitted as extra ground-floor objects or whether they were wholly reducible to sense-data.

Now this way of putting it makes it sound as though philosophers had discovered a new kind of object to which they had given the name 'sense-datum'. Indeed, many of them thought they had. When Paul suggested that it was a misunderstanding of the sense-datum language to infer that philosophers had discovered some new entities, another contributor to the symposium in which he was speaking replied, in amazement at such wrong-headedness, that she had often observed her pupils having the sense-datum experience for the first time! After all, if we are to regard physical objects as logical constructions out of sense-data then sense-data must be a special set of objects; indeed, there will be sense-data or nothing whatsoever, since in a metaphysical sense physical objects will have been eliminated.

The gist of Paul's argument, so far as it concerns us now, is this. If one genuinely discovers a new sort of object, say a virus, or, to use Paul's own example, the fovea in the eye, then thereafter any account of the world which does not mention these objects can be seen to be incomplete. Further, it will be possible to give directions for singling out these objects from the rest, e.g. directions for taking a photograph of the virus with an electron microscope. But, said Paul, this is not the case with regard to sense-data. For those who introduce sense-data say such things as 'If it appears to you that you are seeing a red tomato, then you are having a red sense-datum'. That is, if it appears to you that you see a red tomato then it is *logically necessary* that you are having (sensing) a red sense-datum. This may be contrasted with 'If you look through such a telescope in such a direction you will probably see such and such a star'. Genuine discoveries are not logical consequences of what is already known. What philosophers have in fact done is to introduce a new expression 'having a sense-datum' which is defined in terms of the way objects look. To talk about sense-data will therefore be just another way of talking about the way objects look. That sense-data are a verbal novelty rather than a factual discovery becomes even clearer if we consider such problems about them as 'Can we see the same sense-datum twice?', 'Can the same sense-datum be seen by two different people?', 'What is to count as one and what as two sense-data?'. No amount of looking at the world will help us to answer these questions— all we can do is to make decisions which tighten up the rules for the use of the expression 'sense-datum'.

So much for the philosophical 'discovery' of sense-data. If we turn now to the question of the reduction of physical objects to sense-data, Paul allows that if someone thinks he sees an elliptical-looking penny when there is really no penny there, he *can* say: 'What I really saw was a sense-datum which was elliptical, but was not a sense-datum "of" a penny.' But, he adds, 'It is equally good to say "It only seemed to me as if there was a round penny which looked elliptical. I was really not seeing anything at all." This says just the same thing as the statement which contained the word "sense-datum", and there is no question of the one saying it less or more adequately than the other.' This last sentence is not in the true spirit of reductive analysis. Paul concluded the section of the paper with which we are here concerned with the following paragraph:

My intention has not been to deny that there are sense-data, if by that is meant that (1) we can understand, to some extent at least, how people wish to use the word 'sense-datum' who have introduced it in philosophy, and that (2) sometimes statements of a certain form containing the word 'sense-datum' are true, e.g., 'I am seeing an elliptical sense-datum "of" a round penny'. Nor do I wish to deny that the introduction of this terminology may be useful in helping to solve some philosophical problems about perception; but I do wish to deny that there is any sense in which this terminology is nearer to reality than any other which may be used to express the same facts; in particular I wish to deny that in order to give a complete and accurate account of any perceptual situation it is necessary to use a noun in the way in which 'sense-datum' is used, for this leads to the notion that there are entities of a curious sort over and above physical objects which can 'have' sensible properties but cannot 'appear to have' sensible properties which they have not got.

We might generalize what Paul says, without his authority, in some such way as this: if two sentences are equivalent to each other, then while the use of one rather than the other may be useful for some philosophical purposes, it is not the case that one will be nearer to reality than the other. This is to abandon the whole conception of analysis as a reduction of the world to its basic indubitable constituents. We can say a thing this way and we can say it that way, sometimes; if we can it may be helpful to notice it. But it is no use asking which is the logically or metaphysically right way of saying it.

Thus we have traced the history of the analytic movement, and in particular the theoretical justifications of it, from the time of Russell's first formulation of logical atomism with its scientific philosophical method of analysis, analysis which was to have a success denied to earlier analytic ventures through the new-found powerful techniques of mathematical logic, to its virtual abandonment at the end of the thirties. We have seen it abandoned for reasons which are clearly akin to those which would now be used against it, in favour of aims and methods which are akin to the aims and methods of the philosophers of the present day whose background it has been our aim to explore. It is true that some have continued to apply the title 'analysts' to those who practise the new methods; but that there is a decisive break is evident, and we have reached the end of the period which we set out to survey. It is no part of our aim to praise, criticize, or even to expound the methods of philosophy which replaced the old analysis and are still employed.

RETROSPECT

IT would be impossible to summarize the history of a period already presented in very summary form. But if it be asked how and why the changes which we have noted took place, perhaps the best single answer would be that the other changes were the result of a change in the way language was thought to function. Certain views and presuppositions about the nature of language essential to logical atomism and the view of analysis associated with it were abandoned, with a consequential change in the rest of the philosophical position. In this retrospect we shall examine some of these views and presuppositions and note some of the errors detected in them, though it would not be possible to go fully into all the problems raised.

In particular we shall consider four preconceptions of the atomists regarding language:

(i) In spite of the theory of descriptions the analysts retained what was essentially a *unum nomen, unum nominatum* view of the function of words.

(ii) They regarded a language as having the same character as a logical or mathematical calculus, with constants substituted for variables.

(iii) They thought that language had meaning through a structural similarity of sentence and fact, and that the criterion of perfection in a language was overt similarity of structure.

(iv) They thought that all uses of language which had and could interest the philosopher were of the same kind as descriptions of particular states of affairs.

Of these, the latter three were consciously subscribed to; the first they would probably have denied as a malicious slander.

We had better commence, therefore, by attempting to explain and justify the ascription of such a preconception to them.

Meinong and his followers had held the view *unum nomen, unum nominatum*, the view that every noun must be the name of something having some sort of being, quite explicitly. Russell himself had said that 'being is a general attribute of everything, and to mention anything is to show that it is'.[1] If there was no existent object that a noun named then it must name some subsistent object, or an object having some kind of being other than existence. Now, as Russell early realized, the results of adhering firmly to this doctrine were repugnant to common sense. He was therefore compelled to abandon the doctrine that every noun or noun-like phrase named something; we cannot attribute this simple version of the *unum nomen, unum nominatum* view to him after the earliest phase. Russell came to the conclusion that one could eliminate some nouns and noun-phrases from the language and still say everything that one needed or was entitled to say. These eliminable nouns and noun-phrases, which need not be supposed to have an entity corresponding to them, Russell called descriptions, and we earlier noted briefly the method of analysis he used for dealing with them. Thus Russell was led to the idea that if one carried out this work of elimination by translation systematically one would eventually end with an uneliminable residue of nouns which must be those which genuinely stood for some entities. A combination of this view with empiricism leads straight to the conclusion that the uneliminable terms will be those which name the elements of the given. This immediately provides us with the whole programme of reductive analysis.

But what we must now notice is that though in a way this is an abandonment of the *unum nomen, unum nominatum* doctrine, yet in another way it is a mere variation on that doctrine; it presupposes essentially the same view of the function of

[1] *Principles of Mathematics*, para. 427.

language. It is still maintained that to each genuine *nomen* there corresponds a *nominatum*; in a perfect language, indeed, the doctrine of *unum nomen, unum nominatum* would be true, since all the descriptions of natural languages would there have an explicitly predicative form. We escape the plethora of objects admitted by Meinong and the early Russell quite simply, though there is a suspicion of a conjuring trick about it. Basically we say that unless the supposed object we are dealing with is there, really exists, then, in a correct acceptation of the word 'name', it cannot be named. Only objects of acquaintance are capable of being named, and only logically proper names are, except for the most superficial purposes of grammar, genuine names. Thus instead of preserving the doctrine of *unum nomen, unum nominatum* by freely admitting odd types of object to correspond to every noun or noun-phrase, as Meinong did, we preserve it by not recognizing a (grammatical) noun as a name unless it stands for something whose existence we are prepared to admit. Russell's theory of descriptions does not therefore in fact alter the older view of the way in which names function; it simply re-classifies as descriptions rather than names those names which led to Meinong's metaphysical underworld. Russell is merely more economical in his recognition of entities *and* names than was Meinong: there is no change in the view of names.

Not merely was the ancient linguistic superstition of *unum nomen, unum nominatum* thus in essence retained, but an absurd doctrine of the nature of names was attached to it. Mill had held that a proper name has denotation but no connotation; that is to say, a proper name is used to refer to a thing but has not got a sense, a meaning. No doubt there is something in this intelligently interpreted; we do use the name 'Russell' to refer to something, and it is plainly not possible to ask for the meaning of 'Russell' except in an irrelevant etymological way; again, though one needs to recognize what a thing is like to make sure that one uses the appropriate name of it, if it has one, the name is logically independent of the characteristics of the thing named. We do not need to wait for a baby to be born before we decide what name to give it, though we choose one for a possible boy, one for a possible girl. But to enter the name 'Mary' on the birth certificate of a boy would be a social blunder rather than a mis-statement, as if we put 'female' in the appropriate column. But Russell, following Frege,[1] appears to have thought that an ordinary proper name, which is frequently applied, acquires as its meaning those characters to which we refer in making sure that we correctly apply it. Consequently the doctrine that proper names denote but do not connote was so interpreted that to name a thing was to christen it; but one never could use the name again as a name after the christening ceremony. As it was only sense-data which could be named this was perhaps inevitable in any case, for one never has the same sense-datum twice. It was as if children always died immediately after being christened. But there was also the false logical doctrine that if not used in the christening manner the name inevitably degenerated into a description. Thus Russell maintained that the ordinary proper name 'Socrates' was a disguised description, being equivalent to 'the master of Plato' or 'the philosopher who drank the hemlock'; he apparently did not see that though one might discover that a person was Socrates by discovering that he was the master of Plato the name in fact functions in a very different manner from the description. Ordinary proper names do not degenerate into descriptions after their one proper use at a christening ceremony; the christening ceremony, indeed, is not a use of the name at all, but merely the way in which we give it a use.[2]

[1] See, for example, 'On Sense and Reference' in *Frege Translations*, ed. Black and Geach, esp. pp. 57–58.

[2] The reader is recommended to consult the excellent discussion of Russell's theory of definite descriptions in Strawson's *Introduction to Logical Theory*, Part III, ch. 6, section 10.

Thus it would scarcely be too much to say that the purified and perfect language of the atomists consisted of a set of pseudo-christening ceremonies; pseudo, because they were never to be put to the use to which such ceremonies are dedicated. Further, the only parts of speech which were recognized as possible proper names were those which we call demonstratives, 'this', 'that', and the like. As Russell himself insisted, no atomic proposition was intelligible to a hearer— for how could a christening ceremony of a private sense-datum be informative to anyone? Further, the same proposition became unintelligible to even the speaker when he ceased to contemplate the sense-datum; and one might ask what sense it had ever conveyed to him. So in the end the purification of the language led to something which was admitted to be but doubtfully obtainable in practice and in theory could not be used for any communication. The difficulty is to know why such an oddity should be called a language at all, and what to do with it when one had got it.

The second misunderstanding of language to be considered is the view that language had the same character as a logical calculus, with constants replacing variables. This view was quite explicitly held, with, of course, the reservation that there were other differences due to the imperfections of natural language; such imperfections do not constitute a theoretical difference. Thus Russell said of *Principia Mathematica*: 'It is a language which has only syntax and no vocabulary whatsoever. Barring the omission of a vocabulary I maintain that it is quite a nice language. It aims at being that sort of a language that, if you add a vocabulary, would be a logically perfect language.'[1]

One general ground of this view was the traditional view of the nature of formal logic. Formal logic was conceived as investigating the common formal features of all valid arguments which underlay the variety of subject-matters discussed.

[1] *The Philosophy of Logical Atomism*, Lecture II.

Thus the logicians' syllogism 'If all M is P and all S is M, then all S is P' was thought to embody the formal skeleton common to all arguments which can be made by systematically substituting three common nouns for S, M, and P. If this was the character of formal logic, then it was hard to avoid the conclusion that language is a calculus with an added vocabulary; the calculus is the logical skeleton. The third and fourth preconceptions about language which we have yet to discuss fitted in well with this. For if statements had a structure similar to that of facts, then it was easy to regard the formulae of logic as displaying, bare, the various possible structures; and the view that all uses of language were akin to the making of simple descriptive statements ensured that a logic which seemed adequately to render the one use which had been studied by the logician was a sufficient representative of all.

In spite of differences of comparative detail, such as whether general propositions were concatenations of ordinary descriptions of ordinary particular facts or were ordinary descriptions of an extraordinary sort of general fact, this view was generally accepted without question. Such an insight (though distorted) as Ramsey's, which led him to say that general propositions were not propositions because their use was so different from that of simple descriptive statements, was only an isolated incident. The experiments of the Vienna Circle with new and different calculi did not lead to recognition that there was not this close relationship between languages and calculi; it led merely to the abandonment of the view of the one perfect language corresponding to the one perfect calculus in favour of a multiplicity of possible languages each corresponding to some different calculus. Analysts were unable to recognize that they had misunderstood the relation between languages and formal calculi until they had abandoned their other presuppositions and seen also that reductive analysis, whose possibility had been theoretically explained by taking language to be a truth-functional calculus, was in practice impossible. We cannot embark here on an attempt to give a correct account of the place of formal logic, which must be long and difficult.[1] But the need of a new account was recognized before it was given.

The third misconception of the nature of language was the belief that language had meaning through a structural similarity between sentence and fact stated. It is linked, as we have seen, to that which we have just discussed. It is also linked to the fourth misconception, since it can only be held in combination with a belief that the only meaningful use of language is for the statement of fact. One source of this view is no doubt an over-ready acceptance of the analogy between maps and pictures with language. But another source, perhaps more relevant and more interesting for our purposes, is this. It was recognized, quite rightly, that some sorts of statement and some turns of phrase were more likely to lead to philosophical puzzlement and odd philosophical theories than others; but instead of attributing this to our imperfect command of the concepts we use they attributed it to an inherent rightness in some forms of expression and an inherent wrongness in others. This was normally put in some such way as that in some cases the linguistic form adequately showed the logical form, in some cases did not. But if we are to attribute a logical form to every statement, quite independently of its grammatical form, we have got to explain what we mean. It was very hard not to conclude that the logical form of the statement was a counterpart to the form of the fact, the logical form being more or less adequately displayed by the grammatical form according as the grammatical form of the sentence did or did not approximate to the form of the fact. Linked with the traditional view of the status of formal logic, embodying as it did, from the earliest times, such views as

[1] For such an attempt, very successfully performed, the reader is referred to Strawson's *Introduction to Logical Theory*.

that there was something logically better about such a statement as 'All whales are mammals' than about 'The whale is a
mammal', which was said to require putting into logical form,
this argument seemed irresistible.

There was some virtue in this position; it did involve an
honest effort to explain why one expression was said to be
more imperfect or misleading than another. When the metaphysical oddness of it made philosophers give it up earlier
than any of the other presuppositions we are here considering,
the notion of logical form was for a long time left hanging in
the air. Thus in 1932 Ryle[1] had said: 'I do not see how, save
in a small class of specially-chosen cases, a fact or state of
affairs can be deemed like or even unlike in structure a
sentence, gesture or diagram.' Yet, as we have seen, he still
wished to speak of logical form and to claim that 'Mr.
Baldwin is a politician' better represented the 'real form of
the fact' than did 'Mr. Baldwin is objective'. But it is no
longer clear what this logical form and real form of the fact is
once likeness of structure is rejected. Ryle was then, like so
many others, in an inconsistent stage of transition.

The atomists' belief in clear-cut ready made facts was no
doubt partly due to a desire to avoid the deductions which
their idealist predecessors had drawn from such slogans as
'Knowing affects the known'. But it was partly due also to
this conception of language we are now discussing. There
must be facts with a structure of their own for language to
copy. The truth in the idealist contention was thus missed.
Consider a fact that 'A resembles B more than C'. This was,
in Russell's language, out there in the world (out in the big
world, said Wisdom). A and B may be chairs and C a sofa.
So the chairs resemble each other more than either resembles
a sofa. But if some spectator were more impressed by the
similar upholstery of one of the chairs and the sofa than by
the seating capacity, it would be hard to see how his state-

[1] 'Systematically Misleading Expressions', *Logic and Language*, i, 34.

ment that A (a chair) resembles C (the sofa) more than it resembles B (the other chair) would be wrong. Or we might ask whether a safety razor more resembles a smoothing-plane or a cut-throat razor. For the atomist there was the fact, already there, to give us the answer.

Because of this acceptance of clear-cut facts, to picture which was the task of language, the reclassificatory moves of the metaphysician, as described by Wisdom in his article 'Philosophical Perplexity', were unintelligible to the atomists. Such a statement as 'Time is unreal' seemed to them as either a monstrous denial of such facts as that we had breakfast this morning, or an attempted statement of some supra-sensible fact, or mere raving. Their own metaphysical moves were regarded as analytic and therefore quite different. They did not see that their own reclassificatory moves, such as their thesis that physical objects were logical constructions and not genuine particulars, because physical objects did not answer to their rarified notion of a particular, were not so different from the reclassificatory moves of those who said that time was unreal because it did not answer to their requirements for a genuine substance; in neither case could they diagnose correctly what was being done. Yet if we say, not 'Time is unreal', but 'Time is a logical construction' and not 'Physical objects are logical constructions', but 'Physical objects are not ultimately real', it is hard to see that any important difference has been made to either theory. So long as any genuine use of language is taken to be an attempt to produce a sentence similar in structure to a fact any but the simplest uses of language were inevitably misdescribed.

But this misconception of the function of language was abandoned quite early, though not all the consequences of its abandonment were drawn immediately. We may therefore turn now to what was the most important preconception of all, the fourth, and the last that we shall discuss.

This last presupposition was that all uses of language,

outside mathematics and logic, were essentially similar to its most simple use for reporting particular states of affairs or events. 'This is red', 'This is near that', and 'This hit that', were thought of as being as near to paradigms of linguistic usage as ordinary language could achieve, and not merely as basic empirical statements. Any satisfactory use of language was thought to be a replica or complication of this use. This preconception was the more insidious and dangerous in that it was taken for granted as a commonplace requiring no argument, and, if thought of at all, was regarded as a self-evident truth rather than as a speculation. It was not, of course, a commonplace to think that all genuine statements were empirical, though the logical positivists held this view; but, for example, ethical statements were not thought of as involving a different use of language from that of fact-stating but as recording a special set of facts about a special set of objects; they were perfectly ordinary records of what went on in the world of values. If they were not that they were, as the logical positivists often said, nothing which could interest a philosopher. Similarly metaphysical statements were not regarded as involving a special use of language but as reports of what went on in another (usually better) world outside this cave of appearance in which the non-metaphysician is condemned to live. The various schools of ethical thought, metaphysics and anti-metaphysics, idealism, realism, and sensationalism, did not, in the mind of their adherents, represent different views of what uses of language were possible, but rather different views about the variety of things to be talked about. Thus it could seem to the logical atomist that at the most he had to defend his *precise* view of the nature of fact-stating language and the variety of objects to be described—in other words the precise nature of atomic propositions and their subject-matter.

No doubt it was recognized that exclamations and oaths were not like descriptive statements. But they were regarded

as beneath philosophical notice. Those who thought questions and imperatives important often tried to assimilate
them to statements of the familiar kind; or the optative
'Would that he were here!' was assimilated to 'I wish that he
were here', which was then treated as a piece of descriptive
autobiography.[1] As for such subtlety as the distinction between giving verdicts, telling stories, making claims, consola-
tion, congratulation, promising, all this was hidden by the
blindness which is the guardian angel of preconceptions.

Though, as we have seen, the theory of atomic facts and
propositions degenerates into the ineffable when pressed to
its logical conclusion, the general idea is that an atomic
proposition is something like such English sentences as 'This
is green' or 'This is near that', this sort of statement being the
kind which in suitable circumstances seems least liable to
error, and therefore a suitable basis to which to reduce
human knowledge; also they fitted well with a logical symbolism which could also suffice for '2 is even' or '$2^2 = 4$'. Then,
rather as the object named is the meaning of a name according to Russell's theory of proper names, we think of atomic
facts as the meaning of these atomic propositions. If not
pressed too hard this sort of view of the relation of language
to fact can be made to sound reasonably plausible for statements of this sort and the sorts of words they contain; not
surprisingly, since the view was formed with such statements
in view.

But if we attempt to treat the primitive sort of description
just mentioned as the paradigm of all uses of language,
disaster follows. We ask what fact is stated by a universal
proposition and are puzzled when a general fact, made to
measure, is detected as an obvious imposture, and a whole
set of particular facts, however long the list may be, is always
detected as insufficient; can they then be propositions at

[1] See, for example, F. Kaufmann, *The Methodology of the Social
Sciences*, p. 22.

all, we ask. Metaphysics and moral statements must be thrown overboard by the empiricist; for as there are no metaphysical or moral facts, so there are no metaphysical or moral propositions. Statements about knowledge, belief, wishes, intentions, and hopes could only be kept going by the construction of a psychic machinery, facts about which such statements described, or else by a blatant philosophical behaviourism; that they were descriptions of something could not be doubted. It is because the quest for the meaning of a statement was always interpreted as a request for a translation of it into a form in which it was overtly a description of some process real or imaginary (willing, intending, knowing) that the slogan 'Don't ask for the meaning, ask for the use' could lead to such startling results.

This last presupposition about language was the most stubborn and ingrained of all; in the case of the others common sense was always liable to mitigate the worst effects, even at the cost of consistency. If, inevitably at the cost of distorting oversimplification, we wish to find one single criterion of the conception of philosophy which replaced the old analysis, it would be least inaccurate to find it in the rejection of this presupposition. An attempt to make clear the precise nature of the linguistic procedures implicit in any puzzling expressions without a preconceived classification is the hallmark, not, alas, always deserved, of the newer approach.

But this is an oversimplification, if preferable to some others. An understanding of what is now being done cannot be achieved by any short prescription.

One final warning. We have been dealing largely with theories about the nature of philosophy; such theories are partly attempts to give an explicit description of the methods which the theorist finds embedded in the best practice. But they are usually in part *a priori* theories about what a philosopher should be doing, which may or may not have an effect, not necessarily for the better, on the practice of philosophers. There is interaction between theory and practice. Yet on the whole the best philosophy is little affected by theory; the philosopher sees what needs doing and does it. The reader must not therefore expect all the philosophizing in a given period to conform to the theory, not even that of the theorists. In the end theories must be judged by the practice of the great, dateless works of philosophy; some few of these appeared, in the breach, rather than the observance, of some of the oddest theories, in the period we have been considering.

SOME PRINCIPAL WORKS
DISCUSSED IN THE TEXT

NOTE: this is in no sense a bibliography. It has seemed better to err on the side of brevity, in order to indicate what works are actually discussed in the text and provide some sort of guide to preliminary reading for the less experienced reader.

A. WORKS PRIOR TO LOGICAL ATOMISM

MOORE, G. E., 'The Nature of Judgment', *Mind*, 1899.

RUSSELL, BERTRAND, *The Principles of Mathematics*, Allen & Unwin, 1903.

—— 'On Denoting', *Mind*, 1905.

—— 'Knowledge by Acquaintance and Knowledge by Description', *Proceedings of the Aristotelian Society*, 1910–11.

—— *The Problems of Philosophy*, The Home University Library, Oxford University Press, 1912.

RUSSELL and WHITEHEAD, *Principia Mathematica*, vol. 1, Cambridge University Press, 1910.

B. LOGICAL ATOMISM

MOORE, G. E., 'A Defence of Common Sense', *Contemporary British Philosophy*, second series, edited by Muirhead, Allen & Unwin, 1925.

RAMSEY, F. P., *The Foundations of Mathematics*, Kegan Paul, 1931.

RUSSELL, BERTRAND, *Our Knowledge of the External World*, Allen & Unwin, 1914.

—— 'The Philosophy of Logical Atomism', *Monist*, 1918–19, reprinted by the University of Minnesota.

—— 'Logical Atomism', *Contemporary British Philosophy*, first series, edited by Muirhead, 1924.

STEBBING, S., 'Logical Positivism and Analysis', *Proceedings of the British Academy*, 1933.

—— *A Modern Introduction to Logic*, Methuen, 1930.

—— 'The Method of Analysis in Metaphysics', *Proceedings of the Aristotelian Society*, 1932–3.

WISDOM, JOHN, 'Logical Constructions', *Mind*, 1931–3, in five parts.

WISDOM, JOHN, 'Is Analysis a Useful Method in Philosophy?' *Proceedings of the Aristotelian Society*, supplementary volume for 1933.

—— 'Ostentation', *Psyche*, 1933, reprinted in *Philosophy and Psycho-Analysis*, Blackwell, 1953.

WITTGENSTEIN, L., *Tractatus Logico-philosophicus*, Kegan Paul, 1922.

C. LOGICAL POSITIVISM

AYER, A. J., *Language, Truth and Logic*, Gollancz, 1936.

—— 'Verification and Experience', *Proceedings of the Aristotelian Society*, 1936–7.

—— *Foundations of Empirical Knowledge*, Macmillan, 1940.

CARNAP, R., *Der logische Aufbau der Welt*, Weltkreis-Verlag, 1928.

—— 'The Unity of Science', *Psyche Miniatures*, trans. Black, Kegan Paul, 1934.

—— *Logical Syntax of Language*, Kegan Paul, 1937.

WEINBERG, J., *An Examination of Logical Positivism*, Kegan Paul, 1936.

D. BEGINNINGS OF CONTEMPORARY PHILOSOPHY

AYER, A. J., 'Does Philosophy Analyse Common-Sense?', *Proceedings of the Aristotelian Society*, supplementary volume for 1938.

PAUL, G. A., 'Is there a Problem about Sense-data?', *Proceedings of the Aristotelian Society*, 1936–7, reprinted in *Logic and Language*, Blackwell, 1931.

RYLE, G., 'Systematically Misleading Expressions', *Proceedings of the Aristotelian Society*, 1931–2, reprinted in *Logic and Language*, Blackwell, 1951.

STEVENSON, C. L., 'Persuasive Definitions', *Mind*, 1938.

WISDOM, J., 'Philosophical Perplexity', *Proceedings of the Aristotelian Society*, 1936–7, reprinted in *Philosophy and Psycho-Analysis*, Blackwell, 1953.

—— 'Metaphysics and Verification', *Mind*, 1938, reprinted in *Philosophy and Psycho-Analysis*, Blackwell, 1953.

INDEX

Aristotle, 57–60, 84.
Austin, J. L., 140, 163.
Ayer, A. J., viii, 106, 107, 114-28, 136–48, 157, 167.

Berkeley, G., 38, 42, 43, 94, 100, 101, 118, 154, 155.
Bradley, F. H., 1–4.

Carnap, R., 92, 106, 117–28, 131, 137, 160.
Comte, A., 102.
Constructions, Logical, 36–39, 118, 149 ff., 184.

Descartes, R., 42, 45, 61, 149.

Frege, G., 4, 24, 77, 191.

Generality, 62 ff., 85 ff., 112, 131, 174.

Hahn, H., 106.
Hume, D., 41–44, 94, 98, 102, 107, 108, 116, 118.

Incomplete Symbols, 28–31, 35–38.

Joseph, H. W. B., 84.
Judgement, Moore on, 2; Russell on, 32 ff.

Kant, I., 47, 102.
Kaufmann, F., 198.

Leibniz, G., 5, 16.
Locke, J., 6, 38, 42, 159.

McTaggart, J. E., 40, 42.
Metaphysics, 6, 47–51, 67, 102 ff., 120, 167 ff.
Mill, J. S., 1, 3, 66, 84, 85, 155.
Moore, G. E., vii, viii, 1–4, 35, 36, 48, 50–53, 81, 115, 140, 148, 183.

Negation, 41, 68 ff.
Neurath, O., 106, 122, 123, 137.

Particulars, 17, 54, 58 ff.
Paul, G. A., 183–6.
Picturing facts, 18, 25, 75 ff., 127, 141 ff.
Plato, 41, 118.
Popper, K., 113.
Price, H. H., 147, 183.
Proper names, 17, 28, 82 ff., 139, 189 ff.

Ramsey, F. P., viii, 64–67, 71, 105, 112, 174, 177, 193.
Russell, Earl, Part I *passim*, 99, 106, 112, 130, 135, 138, 149, 150, 182, 183, 187, 189, 190, 192, 195.
Ryle, G., 141–3, 163–6, 195.

Schlick, M., 106, 112, 113, 121.
Spinoza, B., 51.
Stebbing, L. S., 35, 47, 49, 107.
Stevenson, C. L., 170–4.
Strawson, P. F., 133, 191, 194.
Substance, 57 ff., 86.

Truth-functions, 8 ff., 64, 72 ff., 131 ff.

Verification principle, 109 ff., 168 ff., 179.

Waismann, F., viiii, 106, 145, 163.
Weinberg, J., 112.
Whitehead, A. N., 7, 130.
Wisdom, J., viii, 20, 40, 47–50, 55, 65, 70–73, 76–85, 92, 93, 99, 138, 145, 149, 150, 163, 169–82, 195, 196.
Wittgenstein, L., Part I *passim*, 99–111, 116, 122, 127, 132–6, 141, 148, 163, 179.

PRINTED IN
GREAT BRITAIN
AT THE
UNIVERSITY PRESS
OXFORD
BY
CHARLES BATEY
PRINTER
TO THE
UNIVERSITY